ANALYTICAL STUDIES FOR
ENVIRONMENTAL PROTECTION AGENCY

VOLUME IV

Environmental Monitoring

[

A Report to the
U.S. Environmental Protection Agency
from the
Study Group on Environmental Monitoring

Committee on National Statistics
Environmental Studies Board
Numerical Data Advisory Board
Assembly of Mathematical and Physical Sciences
National Research Council

NATIONAL ACADEMY OF SCIENCES
Washington, D.C.   1977

This study was supported by the Environmental Protection Agency.
Contract No. 68-01-2430

Library of Congress Catalog Card Number 77-86463
International Standard Book Number 0-309-02639-3

Available from

Printing and Publishing Office
National Academy of Sciences
2101 Constitution Avenue
Washington, D.C. 20418

Printed in the United States of America

MEMBERS OF THE STUDY GROUP ON ENVIRONMENTAL MONITORING

JOHN W. PRATT *(Chairman)*, Harvard University

WALTER B. LANGBEIN *(Vice-Chairman)*, U.S. Geological Survey
R. STEPHEN BERRY, University of Chicago
RALPH C. d'ARGE, University of Wyoming
MORRIS H. DeGROOT, Carnegie-Mellon University
VIRGIL H. FREED, Oregon State University
JOHN R. KINOSIAN, California Air Resources Board
MARVIN KUSCHNER, State University of New York, Stony Brook
WALTER A. LYON, Pennsylvania Department of Environmental Resources
BRIAN MacMAHON, Harvard University
DAVID E. REICHLE, Oak Ridge National Laboratory

PANEL ON AMBIENT MONITORING

MORRIS H. DeGROOT *(Chairman)*, Carnegie-Mellon University

MYRON B. FIERING, Harvard University
WALTER I. GOLDBURG, University of Pittsburgh
GLENN R. HILST, The Research Corporation
JOHN R. KINOSIAN, California Air Resources Board
WALTER B. LANGBEIN, U.S. Geological Survey
MERVIN E. MULLER, The World Bank

PANEL ON SOURCE MONITORING

WALTER A. LYON *(Chairman)*, Pennsylvania Department of Environmental Resources

FRANCIS J. ANSCOMBE, Yale University
R. STEPHEN BERRY, University of Chicago
PAUL M. BERTHOUEX, University of Wisconsin
VIRGIL H. FREED, Oregon State University
RICHARD W. GERSTLE, PEDCo-ENVIRONMENTAL

PANEL ON EFFECTS MONITORING

MARVIN KUSCHNER *(Chairman)*, State University of New York, Stony Brook

RITA R. COLWELL, University of Maryland

iii

iv

Preface

This report on environmental monitoring is one of a series of studies on the acquisition and use of scientific information in environmental decision making. The studies were performed by the National Research Council for the U.S. Environmental Protection Agency at the request of the U.S. Congress. In this report, we suggest in general terms monitoring that is needed and methods to improve the collection and use of scientific data for environmental management. Environmental monitoring is interpreted broadly to comprise aspects of the collection, analysis, interpretation, and dissemination of scientific data related to environmental problems, whether the data are physical, biological, ecological, or epidemiological.

In addition to collecting some data firsthand, EPA guides monitoring by state, local, and regional agencies. Many of our recommendations are made to EPA. Some, however, are to other organizations that they develop and maintain data that would support EPA's mission. EPA itself should further such efforts by appropriate persuasion, financial sponsorship, or support of legislation.

We have tried to be realistic about EPA's mandate. Some of our recommendations would, however, require changes in legislation or institutions before they could be implemented. If such changes are required, EPA should press for them.

We had to be selective in choosing topics to study. In Chapter 2, the sections on ambient and source monitoring deal mostly with water quality; the section on effects monitoring, with air quality. We have barely touched upon some topics, such as radiation, pesticides, and land use. Others, such as materials damage and global environmental monitoring, were omitted entirely. We also omitted study of noise and of pollutants that may affect stratospheric ozone because other NRC committees were studying them.[1] We concentrated on areas where we thought improvements might be most needed. The reader should not infer that our evaluation of one program in EPA applies to others. For example, the quality assurance programs of EPA for radionuclides are more advanced than those for water quality characteristics. Partly our choices of what to study also reflected the interests and expertise of our members. We examined statistical resources in EPA more closely than those of other scientific disciplines because of our interests as well as because we perceived that EPA understood the relevance of statistics in its work less well than it understood the relevance of other disciplines.

As we point out, the collection of data is very expensive. With regret, however, we decided not to do cost–benefit analyses for our recommended programs. Estimates of costs were generally not available to us, and we did not have the considerable resources that would have been needed to make these analyses responsibly. Neither did we set priorities in all cases. We identified some more important recommendations, and these are underlined in our summary. Sometimes our recommendations can be used to suggest allocation of resources. For example, one scientific principle that too seldom is applied is that better inference can be made from fewer observations carefully collected than from more observations routinely collected with less care. If necessary, some resources for data collection should be reallocated to careful planning and quality assurance. One of our important recommendations is that new monitoring programs, including those that we recommend, should be preceded by prototype studies. These studies should ideally include an analysis of costs versus benefits or, if this is unrealistic, an analysis of cost–effectiveness. For some recommended programs, we discuss explicitly the careful planning needed before the programs are implemented.

One difficulty in assessing costs of monitoring is that details about such expenditures by EPA, other federal agencies, and by state, regional, and local agencies are difficult to obtain. Costs of monitoring are not always tabulated separately in EPA's budget, and many EPA programs have

---

[1]See the following reports: National Research Council (1976) Halocarbons: Environmental Effects of Chlorofluoromethane Release. Report of the Committee on Impacts of Stratospheric Change, Assembly of Mathematical and Physical Sciences. Washington, D.C.: National Academy of Sciences. And: National Research Council (1977) Noise Abatement: Policy Alternatives for Transportation. Report of the Committee on Appraisal of Societal Consequences of Transportation Noise Abatement, Assembly of Behavioral and Social Sciences. Washington, D.C.: National Academy of Sciences.

responsibilities for monitoring. We are unaware of national studies that account for the myriad ambient and source monitoring activities of state and local agencies. From scanty evidence, it appears that, in terms of cost, EPA itself performs no more than one-tenth of the monitoring of air and water quality. In addition, the Agency provides grants to states and local agencies to perform monitoring.

One of our major concerns is the current fragmented assignment of responsibilities for monitoring in EPA. A consequence of this fragmentation is that there is no one in EPA to whom we may address this report other than the Administrator or Deputy Administrator of the Agency.

The choice of monitoring as an area of study by the NRC was made with the encouragement of EPA, which has been working to improve monitoring. Accordingly, some of the factual findings and suggestions we have made may not reflect most recent developments.

The Steering Committee for the Study Group on Environmental Monitoring was appointed by the Committee on National Statistics, the Environmental Studies Board, and the Numerical Data Advisory Board. Members of these NRC sponsoring units guided and assisted us in many ways. We organized our study into three Panels on ambient, source, and effects monitoring, respectively, and invited others to serve on these Panels. Each of the Panels prepared a series of working papers based on their investigations and deliberations, discussed them in meetings, and presented them to the Steering Committee with suggested recommendations. This report is that of the Steering Committee based upon the work of the Panels.

We gathered information through interviews conducted by the Steering Committee and Panels, by some of our members individually, and, mostly, by our staff. We talked with many members of the staff of EPA, the Deputy Administrator, the heads of the Agency's Standing Air and Water Monitoring Work Groups, and many people at EPA headquarters, some regional offices, and laboratories. We also talked with people working in many federal agencies, including the Departments of Agriculture; Health, Education, and Welfare; and Transportation; the National Aeronautics and Space Administration, the National Bureau of Standards, the National Cancer Institute, the National Center for Health Statistics, the National Heart and Lung Institute, the National Institute of Environmental Health Sciences, the National Institute for Occupational Safety and Health, the National Oceanic and Atmospheric Administration, the Tennessee Valley Authority, the U.S. Bureau of the Census, the U.S. Coast Guard, the U.S. Energy Research and Development Administration, the U.S. Geological Survey, the U.S. Occupational Safety and Health Administration, and the U.S. Social Security Administration. In addition, we talked with state and local agencies, industries, private environmental organizations, professional societies, and universities.

An important information gathering activity was a survey of environmental monitoring activities in Allegheny County, Pennsylvania. We sought to identify all types of monitoring activities in the area, the purpose of each activity, the uses and potential uses of data collected, and the adequacy of the monitoring information. Consultants conducted interviews and examined project reports on selected monitoring activities.

We obtained information in several other ways. One consultant prepared a review of health effects monitoring in Europe to help us explore methods that might be adopted in the United States. We conducted a workshop on monitoring the components of industrial processes in order to prevent pollution, in which engineers from several leading industries participated. We solicited information from state environmental protection agencies about their activities in monitoring the effects of pollution directly, and wrote to a number of relevant industries to obtain information about the feasibility of personal monitors. During the course of our study, three relevant conferences were held by others that provided us with information: The Fourth Symposium on Statistics and the Environment (March 1976), an EPA workshop on siting of air pollution monitors (July 1976), and the International Symposium on Environmental Sensing and Assessment (September 1975).

Our report was reviewed by all members of our Study Group, by some members of each of our sponsoring NRC units and the NRC Assembly of Mathematical and Physical Sciences, and by other knowledgeable scientists and engineers suggested by these groups and by us. The reviewers included many with experience in environmental matters; some were from industry. We are very grateful for their advice and helpful suggestions.

As part of this report, the Steering Committee adopted three papers prepared in our Panels; they are included as the first three appendixes. Three other papers, which do not necessarily reflect the views of the Steering Committee, were selected to appear in a supplement to our report. Abstracts of these three papers appear in Appendix E. In Appendix F we list the titles of all papers that were prepared by the members, staff, and consultants to our Panels with information on how these papers and the supplement to our report may be obtained.

Most of the work of this study was done by our staff, and we are grateful to the National Academy of Sciences, especially the Committee on National Statistics, for providing this project with a staff of such high caliber. They gathered the bulk of information for us, summarizing and synthesizing much of it for our review. They participated in our deliberations. They prepared working papers and, what is more important, drafts of the report based upon our deliberations and working papers for our review. Miron L. Straf, as Director, managed the study from the development of the proposal to the completion of this report. The final product owes an enormous debt to his care and skill in editing existent and nonexistent draft material into a report representing, as clearly and accurately as any could, our collective judgments. We were also very fortunate to have J. Stuart Hunter, on sabbatical leave from Princeton University, working especially with the Panels on Source and Ambient Monitoring; Lance A. Wallace, working especially with the Panel on Effects Monitoring; and H. van Olphen, who assisted part time.

We are indebted to a number of consultants. David Rome and Ira Whitman worked closely with us to conduct our survey in Allegheny County. Lester Klashman provided our Panel on Source Monitoring with advice and a paper on water quality monitoring. Dr. Leo Kinlen prepared the review of health effects monitoring in Europe for our Panel on Effects Monitoring.

Claire Chow, Judith Cummings, Barbara Davies, Estelle Miller, and Robert Rooney helped us in editing the report and readying it for publication. Jessica Kaplan assisted throughout the study in many ways, administrative, research related, and secretarial. Barbara Booker also provided secretarial assistance. We thank them and the members of the staff of the Committee on National Statistics for their multifarious work, advice, and assistance.

Finally, we are grateful to all those on the staff of EPA and the other organizations we consulted who gave so willingly of their time and effort.

JOHN W. PRATT, *Chairman*
May 1977

Contents

Summary

MAJOR CONCLUSIONS

When it was created, EPA was challenged to direct and guide environmental programs while confronted with large gaps in scientific knowledge, constrained by excessively detailed specifications in legislation, and hampered by its own fragmented formation and inheritance. The Agency had to establish its programs at great speed. Certain directions it had to take were obvious, and the development of integrated and efficient scientific monitoring programs could not receive priority. Now, however, information from monitoring is essential to the formulation, implementation, and evaluation of environmental management policies to protect human health and well-being at acceptable cost. EPA should take a comprehensive look at monitoring and work toward improvement of its own monitoring programs and those that support its mission in other agencies. The Study Group on Environmental Monitoring finds EPA's current monitoring programs seriously deficient in three major ways.

INADEQUATE USE OF SCIENTIFIC PRINCIPLES

First, EPA does not adequately apply scientific principles to the design, operation, and evaluation of monitoring programs. Programs are too often developed hastily in response to the dictates of legislation and enforcement procedures and the exigencies of pollution control management, instead of being based on clear objectives, priorities, and criteria related to a national monitoring system. As a result, current monitoring does not adequately serve the important purposes of evaluating the progress of national environmental programs in terms of changes in environmental quality and of determining relationships among sources of pollution; ambient environmental quality; and effects on humans, animals, and plants.

NEED TO MONITOR FOR ANTICIPATION AND DISCOVERY

Second, EPA's almost exclusive emphasis on monitoring to control sources of pollution, rather than to discover and anticipate environmental problems, meets only short-term goals. EPA needs to take care of the environment over the longer term, and this responsibility involves more than controlling effluents. It involves, at the least, detecting new environmental problems in early stages, and, at best, anticipating them before they occur. Monitoring programs must be designed to help in understanding causes of pollution, to measure trends in levels of residuals, and to keep watch on the responses of humans, animals, and plants to changes in environmental quality. Without monitoring programs designed for these purposes, the nation is too frequently surprised by environmental crises, and it responds hastily with special studies and hurried legislation, regulations, and enforcement programs. These responses result in monitoring and control policies that are less efficient than they could be.

FRAGMENTATION OF MONITORING

Third, responsibilities for monitoring are fragmented. There is inadequate coordination of monitoring among local, state, regional, and federal agencies, and even among EPA programs themselves. Separate programs often exist where a single program could serve multiple needs; pollutants are measured in one medium that are not measured in others; data on water pollution are collected that are not accompanied by data on flow; and the synthesis of pollution data and the study of relationships between pollution and its effects are hindered by incompatible data collection and processing methods. And because knowledge from disparate scientific disciplines relevant to monitoring is not sufficiently integrated, many types of scientific expertise are absent from the design and evaluation of monitoring systems. The result is that monitoring programs are designed and operated with little or no assessment of their contribution to a national monitoring system or to the success of an overall national environmental program.

RECOMMENDATIONS

SCIENTIFIC LEADERSHIP

Along with significant gaps in environmental monitoring, there is a proliferation of uncoordinated, inefficient, and inflexible monitoring programs that produce data of poor or unknown quality. We conclude that a basic reason for these problems is that environmental sciences in EPA lack leadership in positions that could influence monitoring. Particularly in sciences of environmental monitoring, scientific leadership in the Agency should be developed and given organizational support.

• *We recommend that, within the EPA Administrator's office, an Office of Science be established to exert scientific leadership in EPA, to aid its programs by better integration of scientific principles, and to improve data collection by more scientific influence and direction.* (See Chapter 4.)

If an Office of Science is not established, other means should be found to assure that scientific principles are applied to the design, operation, and evaluation of monitoring programs. From our examinations of a number of monitoring activities, we conclude that EPA's current management of monitoring does not accomplish these important objectives.

EPA's role in the design of ambient water quality monitoring networks is an example of inadequate application of scientific principles. EPA has proposed new networks to replace a current one without evident analysis of the existing network to justify the change. Valuable research is supported by the Agency, including research on monitoring network design, but rarely are the findings applied.

Most monitoring of ambient environmental quality is done by state and local agencies. It is neither necessary nor desirable for EPA to collect all data firsthand, but it is essential that the definition of objectives and the resolution of primary questions of monitoring network design, data management, quality assurance, and cost–effectiveness be the concerns of EPA's central office. We propose that these responsibilities be among those assumed specifically by the Agency's Office of Science.

USE OF PROTOTYPES

Prior to establishing or changing either a data collection procedure of a national monitoring program or a data processing operation, EPA should develop and evaluate prototypes to ensure that data will effectively meet specified needs.

• *We recommend that EPA, through its Office of Science, base its proposals and designs for ambient monitoring networks on prototype studies developed in cooperation with other federal agencies and the states.* (See Chapter 2.)

MANAGEMENT OF SCIENTIFIC DATA

Evaluation of Data Collection and Processing

Fragmentation of monitoring activities within EPA is most evident from the proliferation of separate and uncoordinated data processing and information handling systems. (See Chapter 3.) It is unclear how most of the data in these systems are related to EPA decision making.

• *We recommend that a review and evaluation be made for each current and proposed data processing or information handling system of the Agency in conjunction with its associated monitoring programs. (See Chapter 3.) This review requires that EPA answer the basic questions: Who are the beneficiaries of the data and the system, and what are the specific benefits? How do the data and the system contribute to environmental management, and what high priority needs of the Agency do they meet?*

This review demands work by a full-time professional group, not by part-time advisory groups alone. The review should be among the duties of the Office of Science.

Obtaining Better Measurements

The fledgling quality assurance activities of EPA are uncoordinated and inadequately funded. Those responsible have little authority to see that uniform definitions and protocols are used. More and broader national programs of interlaboratory comparisons are needed to determine the accuracy of data on environmental characteristics and to maintain accuracy and stimulate improvements. Until these deficiencies are corrected, most of the data on which policies ought to be based will be of poor or unknown accuracy.

• *We recommend that a continuing certification program be established for those laboratories that, by performing measurements, determine whether industries and state and local governments are complying with permits or standards.* (See Chapter 3.)

Such certification should be based on performance and not solely on evaluations of personnel, equipment, and methods.

Pollution control strategies are often developed from inventories based on an enumeration of sources and estimates of emissions from them. Thus, mistakes in these inventories can be costly. EPA should develop a source inventory quality assurance program to evaluate different methods for compiling inventories and to provide standard definitions of sources.

For each pollutant that EPA requires to be monitored, the Agency establishes a reference measurement method, an authorized protocol for sampling and measuring a level of concentration. As part of this procedure, EPA should study alternative measurement methods to determine their compatibility and to develop ways of relating the results of one method to those of another.

Data Analysis and Dissemination

If it is to make informed decisions, EPA should analyze the data it acquires. It appears, however, that most of these data are not analyzed adequately. Since data collection is expensive, EPA should determine that data not only meet their intended purposes efficiently but that they serve as many purposes as possible. The Agency should analyze its environmental data in relation to various purposes they could serve, such as evaluating national monitoring networks, measuring the progress of environmental programs, and studying relationships between pollution and its effects. In addition, EPA should summarize its data in more informative annual reports and disseminate data earlier and more widely to others who would find them helpful. EPA research reports, at least those that may have a major impact on public policy, should undergo external scientific review, and some should be submitted to refereed journals. The Agency should also publish the scientific and economic analyses upon which its decisions are based.

Statistical Resources in EPA

The problems with EPA's management of scientific data are exacerbated by the paucity of statistical talent in the Agency. In addition to producing and consuming data about the environment, EPA has many statistical responsibilities. For example, the Agency writes environmental guidelines and standards that must take account of natural variability, and it specifies statistical measures in regulations that must be designed for efficient enforcement. Statisticians are needed to cooperate with other scientists in improving the design of experiments and surveys and in improving techniques for sampling, data analyses, quality assurance, and decision making under uncertainty. EPA should develop, particularly in its Office of Science, sufficient talent to meet its many statistical responsibilities.

Some of our recommendations are that organizations other than EPA develop and maintain data that would be used in support of EPA's mission. EPA itself should further these efforts by appropriate persuasion, financial sponsorship, or support of legislation.

Health Effects of Air Pollution

A long-term epidemiological study is needed to measure the health benefits of air pollution control. Many difficulties must be faced: the design of the study should consider the accuracy and relevance of measurements of both health and the environment, the high correlations among levels of many pollutants, and the effect of omitting pollutants that contribute to harmful effects. EPA should not be solely responsible for such a complex enterprise.

• *We recommend that careful planning begin immediately among various agencies most involved for a long-term, multi-city study of the effects of air pollution on human health, including both chronic and acute disease.* (See Chapter 2.)

For estimating the exposure of the population, the study should pay special attention to the use of personal monitors and mobile vans, along with models, to supplement fixed stations. We also recommend that EPA support the development of personal air pollution monitors and move toward further measuring and reporting the respirable fraction of particulate matter.

Monitoring to Anticipate Pollution Problems

We considered ways in which programs to monitor the components and expected wastes of industrial processes, the transportation of possibly hazardous substances, and the operation of wastewater treatment plants could provide information to anticipate pollution problems.

No programs currently require industry to monitor the components of its manufacturing processes even though, in many cases, industry is already capable of doing so. Such monitoring could detect changes from routine operations and thereby provide warning of unusual types of residuals or increased levels of familiar residuals so that their environmental effects could be anticipated and diminished. The practice should be fostered.

In addition, before a new product is manufactured or a new process instituted, industry should analyze the expected waste to identify the substances that will be discharged and to assess their potential effect on the environment. The information should be made available to EPA and state environmental protection agencies.

Current efforts by federal agencies to prevent transportation accidents that cause pollution are inadequate. Although EPA may regulate the transportation of hazardous wastes, no federal agency has the authority to require carriers to report their plans for transporting other possibly hazardous chemicals. Routine reporting is not needed, but rather the authority for an agency to monitor transport when and where it poses a danger to the public. In addition, EPA and carriers should formulate guidelines and plans for the safe transport of potentially hazardous substances. At the least, bills of lading for such substances should include the scientific name of chemicals being shipped.

In view of evidence that many municipal wastewater treatment plants are not operating as designed, EPA should provide better monitoring procedures and technical assistance for evaluating the efficiency of such plants and for determining whether problems are due to overloading, management, or design. EPA could thus improve the design and operation of treatment plants and determine whether, in achieving water quality standards, it is more efficient to allocate resources to municipal sewerage systems for operation and maintenance than for construction.

Monitoring to Discover Environmental Problems

We recommend a number of programs to improve EPA's ability to discover environmental problems early by keeping timely watch on changes in environmental quality and the responses of humans, animals, and plants (see Chapter 3). Determining changes requires the establishment of a base from which to measure.

Baseline Monitoring The discovery of the toxic effects of many chemicals leads to questions concerning their occurrence in the environment. Base levels for many of these chemicals could be established, ideally, with a quantitative assessment now of parts of the environment that could be scrutinized years later to detect the presence of chemicals that proved to have adverse effects. With modern techniques, such as gas chromatography and mass spectrometry, analytical records of selected samples can be preserved.

• *We recommend that EPA analyze samples of the environment for the presence and quantity of selected chemicals and preserve analytical records for retrospective analyses of other chemicals.*

Samples of air, water, soil, and biota should be periodically collected from various regions and analyzed. Gas chromatograms and mass spectrograms should be preserved for retrospective analyses of chemicals that subsequently are suspected to have adverse effects. (See Chapter 2.)

There is evidence that acidic precipitation has been increasing in some areas of the United States and that it has a number of deleterious effects. It may leach nutrients from the soil and impede the growth of vegetation; it may reduce the abundance and diversity of fish and micro-flora and fauna of rivers and lakes; and it may increase the corrosion of materials.

• *We recommend the establishment, following prototype studies, of a national network to monitor the acidity and other characteristics of precipitation and particulates that fall to earth.* (See Chapter 2.)

Surveillance of Humans A promising activity of monitoring for discovery is surveillance to detect changes in human mutation rates. Findings of no increase in mutation rates would provide reassurance. Findings of increased mutation rates would provide evidence for the regulation of man-made mutagens and might need to be followed by studies to determine causal agents. Monitoring genetic effects in humans is now technically feasible, but many important problems remain to be studied. We recommend that research policy conferences be sponsored to discuss the scientific, social, and cost–benefit problems of monitoring for genetic effects in humans.

To aid in the discovery of new environmental risks, a disease detection program should be established, based on continuing surveillance of particular groups of people who are or have been exposed to chemicals known to be animal carcinogens but not yet identified as human carcinogens. Exposure may sometimes be defined by body burden, the level of substances accumulated within the body.

We recommend programs to improve health statistics and facilitate epidemiological studies, so that environmental hazards may be discovered early and dose-response relationships of pollutants better determined. Long-term epidemiological studies are often impeded by difficulties in establishing the fact of death and determining which state has recorded the death certificate. We recommend that a National Death Index be established to provide this information. (We recognize that facilitating access to already available information involves some loss of privacy.) In addition, there should be further study of the comparability and completeness of occupations reported on death certificates and in the census.

Since most pollutants that impair health may first be discovered in the industrial environment, where exposure is intense and relatively uncomplicated by other pollutants, the possibility should be explored of making occupational health statistics more useful for studying the effects of environmental hazards. Employee work records should be retained by employers for a length of time sufficient to permit epidemiological studies. There may be a need to compare different records for the same individual in order to follow and relate occupational, residential, and medical history. An interagency task force should weigh the benefits of this and other comparisons of records against their monetary and social costs, which include possible invasions of privacy.

Surveillance of Animals and Plants Monitoring for surveillance of animals and plants should include productivity, diversity, fecundity, bioaccumulation, and other important aspects of biological species on plots in natural ecosystems; and productivity of major agricultural crops, forage, and forests on selected field plots. In addition, periodic regional surveys should be made of those biological species, including microorganisms, that indicate trends in environmental quality.

• *We recommend that EPA coordinate and support long-term monitoring of certain natural, managed, and damaged ecosystems to identify and assess chronic effects of environmental quality.*

COORDINATION OF MONITORING ACTIVITIES

An Office of Science would facilitate coordination of environmental monitoring activities, especially among EPA and state and local agencies, by working cooperatively with them to improve monitoring. Some of the current fragmentation of monitoring is the result of legislation in which Congress has included excessively detailed specifications for data collection.

• *We recommend that monitoring information and reporting requirements imposed by legislation and EPA regulations be reviewed and changes suggested in those that decrease the effectiveness of monitoring programs or impose unnecessary costs. EPA should conduct such a review cooperatively with federal, state, and local agencies.* (See Chapter 4.)

Data relevant to environmental management are collected by many federal agencies. Their efforts must be coordinated, particularly so that data on environmental quality can be related to data on health and ecological effects and so that EPA can monitor the responses of humans, animals, and plants to changes in environmental quality. EPA alone, however, cannot provide this coordination.

• *We recommend that a National Committee on Environmental Monitoring be established to coordinate federal environmental monitoring efforts.* (See Chapter 4.)

Introduction

In 1970, when EPA was established, some of the major pollution problems were obvious, and it was clear in which directions the Agency had to take its first steps. Since then the discovery of the toxic effects of many chemicals, the possible chronic effects of some pollutants at low concentrations, the synergistic effects of combinations of pollutants, and the increases in one form of pollution that result from abatement of another have made current regulatory efforts to protect the environment more complex. Data on environmental quality and the effects of pollution are now essential in formulating, implementing, and evaluating sound environmental decisions. Sound policy decisions are important, because environmental management is expensive; the Council on Environmental Quality reports that, in terms of 1975 dollars, annual public and private pollution control expenditures will rise from $31.7 billion in 1975 to $69.2 billion in 1984 (CEQ 1976). In addition, there is increasing reason to be concerned about inadequate knowledge regarding environmental hazards. There are now many more types of chemicals in the environment; their ubiquity is recognized; people have been exposed to them longer; and the capacity of the environment to assimilate them has presumably been reduced.

EPA was challenged to direct and guide environmental programs while confronted with large gaps in scientific knowledge, constrained by excessively detailed specifications in legislation, and hampered by its own fragmented formation and inheritance. EPA had to establish its programs at great speed in a rapidly changing climate of opinion about the environment. In its first years, the Agency could not give priority to the development of integrated and efficient scientific monitoring programs capable, in particular, of evaluating the progress of national environmental programs in terms of improved environmental quality and of determining relationships among sources of pollution, ambient environmental quality, and effects on humans, animals, and plants. Now, however, it is time for EPA to take a comprehensive look at monitoring and to improve its programs.

At present, there are significant gaps in environmental monitoring, as well as a proliferation of uncoordinated, inefficient, and inflexible programs that produce data of poor or unknown quality. Monitoring does not serve the important purpose of providing information to guide the formulation and aid the implementation of national policies for environmental management. Too often monitoring programs are developed, not according to scientific principles, but in hasty response to the dictates of legislation, enforcement procedures, and the exigencies of pollution control management. We conclude that a basic reason for these problems is inadequate scientific leadership within EPA to establish objectives, priorities, and criteria, and to guide other policies of environmental monitoring in ways that are useful in the design and evaluation of monitoring systems.

Throughout our report, we point to the need for better use of science within EPA. The current fragmented assignment of responsibilities for monitoring within the Agency does not provide for adequate attention to these important matters. Some unit with sufficient authority, scientific capability, and experience in environmental problems needs to be assigned overall responsibility in EPA for assuring that scientific principles are applied to the design, operation, and evaluation of monitoring systems. Because data collection is expensive (in Chapter 3 we estimate that the cost for one air monitoring station is $40,000 per year), the cost–effectiveness of monitoring in relation to the use of the information is an integral part of the scientific approach to monitoring, and the improvement of cost–effectiveness would be an important concern of such a unit.

To assume these and other responsibilities, we propose in Chapter 4 that an EPA Office of Science be established to advise the Administrator on science policy and to provide scientific focus and leadership for the Agency. A number of specific functions related to monitoring, which would naturally be assigned to this Office, are discussed in Chapters 2 and 3. The Office of Science is, of course, mentioned in those discussions, but its full treatment is deferred to Chapter 4. Whether or not our recommendation for a new office is adopted, EPA should address the problems we discuss in Chapters 2 and 3.

REFERENCE

Council on Environmental Quality (1976) Environmental Quality: The Seventh Annual Report of the Council on Environmental Quality. Washington, D.C.: U.S. Government Printing Office.

1 An Overview of Current Environmental Monitoring Activities

TYPES OF MONITORING

Man's activities affect natural phenomena, and the resulting changes affect man. Environmental monitoring refers to repeated observations for study of these relations. The objective of environmental monitoring is to guide the formulation and aid the implementation of environmental management policies designed to protect human health and well-being, which includes ecological well-being.

Monitoring activities can be divided into three categories, each designed to answer different questions:

Source Monitoring. What residuals enter or will enter the environment? From what sources and in what amounts?

Ambient Monitoring. What concentrations of residuals are present in air, water, soil, food, and animal tissues?

Effects Monitoring. What are the consequences of these residuals for humans, animals, plants, and materials?

Source monitoring serves in enforcing compliance with emission standards; forecasting those activities of production, storage, transportation, use, and disposal that may cause pollution; and taking inventory of emissions from production processes. Ambient monitoring serves in determining changes in levels of current and potential pollutants in the environment, inspecting for compliance with standards of ambient concentrations of pollutants, and gathering information for understanding the transport and distribution of residuals. Effects monitoring serves in determining the impacts of current and potential pollutants on humans, animals, plants, and materials and evaluating their economic, social, and aesthetic costs.

SOURCE MONITORING

Sources of residuals in the environment may be classified as point sources, area sources, and mobile sources.

POINT SOURCES

Industrial stacks, discharge pipes, and other stationary sources that contribute residuals to air, water, and land are called point sources. State authorities prepare inventories of point sources that include the location of the source, the pollutants emitted, and estimates of the amount emitted. Data from inventories of sources of air pollution are reported to an EPA data bank called the National Emissions Data System (NEDS). These and other data are used by managers of Air Quality Control Regions to predict ambient air quality. Emergency steps of a control plan may be initiated if an air pollution episode is predicted. Inventories of water pollution sources are used to develop plans for waste-treatment facilities and to determine appropriate effluent limitations ("waste load allocations") required to maintain ambient water quality standards.

Most source monitoring is done by individual dischargers. Those who discharge residuals into waters must obtain a National Pollutant Discharge Elimination System (NPDES) permit from EPA or a state authorized by EPA to issue these permits. Such permits specify how a discharge is to be monitored. Dischargers of air pollutants must meet New Source Performance Standards if they establish a new process or plant after EPA has issued regulations for their industry. State agencies also monitor sources of air and water pollution to assure compliance with permits and standards, and to prepare inventories of point sources.

Local agencies are required by EPA to monitor the discharges from industry into municipal waste-treatment plants, as well as the discharges from waste-treatment plants. Analysis of such industrial wastes determines user charges and appropriate levels of waste treatment.

AREA SOURCES

Area or nonpoint sources are groupings of small sources spread over regions, such as cities, farmlands, or forests. Area-source monitoring is being initiated by state and local agencies as part of areawide waste treatment management plans that are required by legislation. The amount of residuals in rivers and streams from area sources is often inferred from demographic and industrial statistics. Land-use inventories, which are also used for this purpose, are prepared by the U.S. Geological Survey (USGS) and the U.S. Department of Agriculture (USDA). Some area sources of water pollution, such as feed lots and mines, must have EPA NPDES permits that require self-monitoring. The systematic monitoring of residuals from rangeland, forests, farmlands, and mines is in a formative stage.

MOBILE SOURCES

Pollution from mobile sources includes motor vehicle emissions and spills of toxic and other hazardous substances during transport. EPA monitors both new and old cars to determine levels of emissions. The U.S. Department of Transportation monitors pollution caused by spills of hazardous substances being transported by aircraft, trucks, buses, railroads, and pipelines; the U.S. Coast Guard in that Department monitors spills from barges and other waterborne vessels.

AMBIENT MONITORING

Ambient monitoring refers to the measurement of concentrations of pollutants in the air, water, soil, and biota.

AIR

State and local agencies perform most of the ambient air monitoring. The number of stations, pollutants measured, and other details are developed in a state implementation plan (SIP), which must be approved by EPA and must meet certain minimum requirements specified by EPA. For example, EPA specifies a minimum number of stations for each of the nation's 247 Air Quality Control Regions in order to monitor the six criteria air pollutants for which EPA has established National Ambient Air Quality Standards (NAAQS). In addition, EPA specifies the measurement methods that may be used. States usually operate more monitoring stations and monitor more pollutants than EPA requires;

about 8000 stations are operated by states. The data are reported to the EPA National Aerometric Data Bank (NADB) and are available through an EPA computer system called Storage and Retrieval of Aerometric Data (SAROAD). The principal national ambient air quality network is the National Air Surveillance Network (NASN), a system that generally allocates one station to each major urban area and consists of about 400 stations. The network, begun in the 1950s by the Public Health Service and continued by the National Air Pollution Control Administration, a predecessor of EPA, is now operated by EPA in cooperation with state and local agencies.

Another national monitoring system operated by EPA is the Community Health Air Monitoring Program (CHAMP), a system of about 20 stations measuring both criteria and noncriteria pollutants in several cities for the purpose of research on health effects of air pollution. EPA also operates the Regional Air Monitoring System (RAMS), a St. Louis area network of about 25 stations established to study transportation and transformation of pollutants.

In addition to these governmental systems, some large industries monitor ambient levels in their neighborhoods. The extent of industrial monitoring is not known: a recent EPA inventory[1] located over 600 stations operated by industry measuring sulfur dioxide alone.

WATER

The federal agencies with major responsibility for ambient water quality monitoring are USGS and EPA. About 30,000 water quality monitoring stations are operated by the states and by USGS. Two national networks have recently been established: the National Stream Quality Accounting Network (NASQAN), a set of stations (525 are expected by 1979) operated by USGS; and an EPA National Water Quality Surveillance System (NWQSS), a set of 70 pairs of stations located upstream and downstream from areas that are sources of pollution. The objective of the first network is to record water flow and pollutant concentrations in a number of water resources planning regions. The presence of selected microorganisms, particularly coliforms, as indicators of pollutants is also monitored in the network. The purpose of the second network is to determine the effects of agricultural or industrial development on water quality. Most water quality monitoring stations are operated by state and local agencies that collect information for their specific needs. EPA

[1]U.S. Environmental Protection Agency (1976) Background and General Considerations in the Development of Strategy Issues for Improvement in Air Monitoring. Draft report (July 30) of the EPA Standing Air Monitoring Work Group.

grants for pollution abatement programs require states to monitor and report ambient water quality. Some of the fixed ambient water quality stations that collect data for state and local agencies are operated by USGS through a cooperative program. Thus, a state that is required by EPA to monitor water quality may ask a USGS district office to design, install, and operate a monitoring network. The cost is shared between the state and USGS. Forty-three states and the USGS report their ambient water quality data to the EPA data bank called Storage and Retrieval for Water Quality Data (STORET).

The Safe Drinking Water Act requires most states and local agencies to monitor and report to EPA on the quality of drinking water. EPA itself measures levels of possibly harmful organics in the drinking water of about 100 cities and radionuclides in drinking water at 76 sites.

TISSUES, SOIL, AND FOOD

A number of ambient monitoring programs measure levels of pesticides, heavy metals, and other substances in humans, animals, and plants. The EPA Human Tissue Monitoring Program measures levels of 19 pesticides and PCBs in samples of tissue collected from autopsies and operations. The U.S. Fish and Wildlife Service measures insecticides, mercury, and other substances in fish, starlings and other birds, and small mammals. Many states also monitor levels of pollutants in tissues of animals and in plants. The USDA and the USGS monitor the erosion of soil and the transport of sediment. EPA measures pesticides in soil as well as in air and water. The U.S. Food and Drug Administration operates a Total Diet Survey (better known as the Market Basket Survey) which measures levels of pesticides and 6 heavy metals in 117 food items comprising the average diet of teenage males.

EFFECTS MONITORING

Unlike the case for source and ambient monitoring, a large portion of the monitoring of effects on humans and the biota is done by federal agencies. Few state and local agencies monitor effects of air pollution, although there are state and local agencies which monitor effects of water pollution on aquatic biota.

EFFECTS ON HUMANS

The major EPA program to monitor the effects of air pollution on human health was the Community Health and Environmental Surveillance

System (CHESS), a series of studies to relate frequency and severity of respiratory illnesses to ambient levels of air pollution. One purpose of CHESS was to evaluate the already established National Ambient Air Quality Standards (NAAQS). A second purpose was to monitor health as controls were applied. The studies were conducted in eight communities from 1969 to 1975 and involved more than 300,000 volunteers. Now, only certain special research studies are conducted.

Other federal agencies collect data on human health that can be correlated with data on pollution or used in other epidemiologic studies. The National Center for Health Statistics (NCHS) collects data on births and deaths from the states, and data on illness and the use of health facilities through four surveys: (1) a continuous Health Interview Survey that secures data on health status and the use of health services through interviews of 130,000 people each year; (2) a series of Health Examination Surveys (at 2- to 5-year intervals) in which probability samples of 7,000 to 30,000 persons are given physical examinations to determine physical, physiological, medical, dental, and nutritional characteristics (some are given tests to determine levels of heavy metals in tissues and blood); (3) annual Ambulatory Care Surveys, in which national sample surveys of physicians are used as the source of data on numbers of visits to physicians according to the reason for the visit (including diagnosis) and the type of treatment provided; and (4) continuing quarterly and annual national probability samples of hospitals, providing data on diagnosis, treatment, and length of stay for 200,000 discharges each year. The National Cancer Institute (NCI) has conducted three cancer morbidity surveys (1937, 1947, and 1969–71) in several states and metropolitan areas. Through its Surveillance Epidemiology and End Results (SEER) program, NCI also operates or funds cancer incidence reporting systems in selected areas, which cover 10 percent of the U.S. population. In addition, there are a few state and local cancer registers. Annual estimates of occupational illness are obtained by the Bureau of Labor Statistics (BLS) for the Occupational Safety and Health Administration (OSHA).

ECOLOGICAL EFFECTS

Federal, state, and local agencies monitor environmental effects on animals and plants. State and local agencies monitor fish and microorganisms to identify and study the effects of water pollution. Federal and state agencies monitor the ecological effects of various kinds of land uses.

The major ecological effects monitoring program of EPA has been the National Eutrophication Survey (1972 to 1975), a study of the effects of nitrates and phosphates on plant life in 800 lakes. Other federal agencies that monitor ecological effects are the USDA, which studies the effects of air pollutants and pesticides on crops; the U.S. Fish and Wildlife Service, which studies the effects on animals; the U.S. Energy Research and Development Administration (ERDA), which studies the ecological effects of pollution from power plants; and the Tennessee Valley Authority, which monitors the effects of sulfur dioxide on vegetation near its power plants.

2 Purposes of Monitoring

NEED FOR IMPROVING MONITORING PROGRAMS

Environmental management is complex. Monitoring is essential to making good environmental decisions. But information from monitoring does not yet sufficiently influence EPA's decisions. One reason is that current federal, state, and, local monitoring programs do not provide the data required to predict the consequences of various environmental management policies, their costs, and their benefits. Data alone, of course, will not solve all problems. For example, in most prediction problems, an understanding of environmental processes is also required.

Another reason is that EPA does not sufficiently depend on monitoring to take proper care of the environment over the longer term. This responsibility requires it to detect environmental problems in early stages, and ultimately to anticipate such problems before they occur. To fulfill this purpose, monitoring programs must be designed to help understand causes of pollution, measure trends in levels of residuals, and keep watch on the responses of humans, animals, and plants to changes in environmental quality. The almost exclusive emphasis of EPA on monitoring to control sources of pollution rather than to discover and anticipate environmental problems meets only short-term goals.

Without monitoring programs designed for these purposes, the nation is too frequently surprised by environmental crises, and it responds hastily with special studies and hurried legislation, regulations, and

21

enforcement programs. These responses result in monitoring and control policies that are less efficient than they could be.

The difficulty in determining relationships among sources of pollutants, ambient environmental quality, and effects on humans, animals, and plants makes careful design of monitoring programs essential. Explicitness and coordination in design are also important if more than limited purposes are to be served.

PURPOSES OF MONITORING AND RELATIONSHIPS AMONG SOURCE MONITORING, AMBIENT MONITORING, AND EFFECTS MONITORING

Evaluation of our national programs to protect the environment and to obtain the knowledge needed for developing future policies and programs has ranked low in EPA's hierarchy of problems. The importance of adequate knowledge in view of the increasing complexity of environmental decisions and trade-offs is already obvious. If the history of other public works, such as flood control and reclamation, is any guide, demands for explicit evaluation of accomplishment will also increase.

Many questions are being and will be raised. To what extent do the results of legislation, regulations, enforcement, and expenditures for waste treatment programs show up in environmental quality? Is there an irreducible minimum of pollution dictated by the number of people and the things they use? Treating residuals in one medium may create new residuals elsewhere (for example, the incineration of sludge from sewage treatment plants, or the dumping on land of solid wastes removed from air pollution control equipment). Are new environmental problems outpacing the resolution of old ones? What is the natural assimilative capacity of lakes and rivers to recycle wastes? How much of water pollution is due to natural contaminants? Monitoring programs will need to relate ambient quality to sources and effects if questions such as these are to be answered.

We do not anticipate that the discovery of these relationships will come easily, but environmental management beyond mere enforcement of compliance with discharge regulations requires this chain of information on residuals. The initial links in the chain are data on the location of sources of pollution and on the amounts and types of pollution produced. Such data are most applicable to pollution control and provide indications of possible subsequent effects on humans and the biota. Their use for environmental management depends on methods to relate sources of pollution to ambient environmental quality. Ambient data occur midway in the chain from sources to effects and, if the relationships between ambient quality and effects have been determined satisfactorily, can provide an early indication of effects that may result. Ambient data, if collected properly, can also help to evaluate the effectiveness of our source control programs. They are not, in our current state of knowledge, substitutes for direct measurement of ultimate effects on human health and the biota.

OBJECTIVES TO GUIDE MONITORING

These broad purposes must be taken into account in the design of monitoring networks. But designing a network that is cost–effective requires one to define specific operational objectives and criteria in advance.

EPA should provide these objectives, but the Agency has thus far failed to take adequate leadership responsibility for them. Legislation, while sometimes prescribing restrictive requirements on monitoring, usually leaves objectives too broad to guide particular monitoring programs. Operational objectives and criteria for the design of a monitoring system should include: (a) purposes of data collection and their uses for governmental and private operations, decisions, analysis, and research; (b) methods of data handling (see Chapter 3 for suggested objectives); (c) institutional responsibilities for monitoring; and (d) statistical and engineering principles for design and evaluation (for example, mass balances).

EPA has, in the past, awarded contracts for "the design of monitoring surveillance systems" which leave the tasks of specifying objectives and constructing design criteria to the contractor. Such studies cannot produce satisfactory results. EPA should understand and specify the criteria to be applied, especially measures of effectiveness and statistical and technical criteria for field sampling and laboratory analysis.

Although EPA cannot be organized on the basis of data collection, the Agency should recognize that information is the basis upon which its decisions and the evaluation of its results depend. It is neither necessary nor desirable for EPA to collect all data firsthand, but it is essential that the definition of both broad and operational objectives and the resolution of primary questions of monitoring network design, data management, quality assurance, and cost–effectiveness be among the concerns of EPA's headquarters. Other functions of EPA should be the continuing evaluation of the cost–effectiveness of monitoring programs, and research to improve the data base. The current fragmented assignment of responsibilities within EPA for monitoring does not provide for adequate attention to these important matters (see Chapter 4). Because we perceive that these tasks are not now being accomplished, we suggest that responsibilities for monitoring be among those assumed specifically by an Office of Science that we propose be established in EPA (see Chapter 4).

SOURCE MONITORING

Environmental degradation begins with sources such as industrial or power plants, vehicles, or farms. Monitoring of sources is in many ways the simplest part of the monitoring process, which becomes more complex as it follows the movement and diffusion of pollutants into the ambient environment and observes their subsequent appearance in and resulting effects on humans, animals, and plants.

INVENTORIES

One of the first tasks in source monitoring is to develop an inventory. An inventory is a catalogue of residuals and their sources, and, usually, of estimates of amounts discharged into the environment, based on measurements or on production activity. An inventory may be used to identify critical stresses on the environment, or to provide data for models of the transport and fate of residuals, or for both purposes.

Three categories of sources of pollutants can be identified (see Chapter 1): stationary or point sources (e.g., industrial, waste-treatment, or power plants); area or nonpoint sources (e.g., urban or agricultural areas); and mobile sources (e.g., motor vehicles or spills during transport). A point source inventory includes the location of each source, the character of its operation, and estimates of the amounts of important residuals emitted. Knowledge of the industrial processes involved and the media that ultimately receive the wastes is desirable for its compilation. Mobile source inventories are based, in part, on motor vehicle registration systems. Traffic surveys provide one approach to quantifying the density of vehicles in a given geographical area at a specific time. For inventories of area sources, the variety of sub-sources presents a major problem in determining amounts of residuals. In an agricultural area, for example, sub-sources of pollution include pesticide use, animal waste, crop waste, soil erosion, burning, and vehicular sources. Here, pollutants directly enter air, water, soil, and biota.

Pollution control strategies are often based on data from source inventories. Thus, mistakes in these inventories can be costly. Most inventories of air pollution sources are based on *emission factors* developed for various industries from information such as the manufacturing process and type of fuel used. In Pittsburgh, a recently revised air pollution source inventory was based on actual measurements. Particulate emissions were estimated to be 50 percent higher than those reported in a previous inventory based on emission factors.

How can the accuracy and completeness of inventories be improved? We find no substitute for a strong inventory quality assurance program within EPA. The Agency should address the following issues:

1. *Different methodologies.* When can emission factors and other estimates replace measurements? Are complete enumerations necessary or would samples suffice? How can undercounts be estimated? How may materials balances provide checks? How can inventories be kept current? Answers to these questions depend on the uses as well as the type of the inventory.

2. *Standardization of definitions.* What constitutes a source? Is it an industrial unit, a component of that unit, or an individual pipe or vent? Some definitions are published in regulations and guidelines. For water pollution, however, there is no commonly agreed upon definition of a source. Those for pesticides and fugitive dust are particularly unclear.

3. *Comparability with other compilations.* It would be helpful if EPA identified categories of limits on sources of water pollution for classes of industries by codes, such as the Standard Industrial Classification (SIC) code, in order to make simple comparisons among water pollutant source inventories prepared by state agencies and EPA. For atmospheric emissions the Agency identifies individual sources by a Source Classification Code (SCC), which is more specific than the SIC code.

PERMIT PROGRAMS

Permit programs, which require self-monitoring by those who discharge pollutants, help ensure compliance with regulations. The most extensive permit program is the National Pollutant Discharge Elimination System (NPDES) established by the Water Pollution Control Act of 1972 and operated by EPA or by states authorized by EPA. Permit programs for emissions into the air are conducted by most states.

The NPDES program applies to point-source dischargers of pollutants to navigable waters and to the ocean. As of September 30, 1976, 19,359 of 21,985 identified municipal sources and 33,364 of 42,892 identifed nonmunicipal sources were issued permits. (In the latter category, 99 percent of the "major" sources were covered.)

The applicant for a permit must submit information on the location, amount, and chemical makeup of the discharge. After his application is approved, he must sample and analyze his effluent periodically (in some cases, continuously or daily), and periodically submit data on specific pollutants to the EPA regional administrator. The residuals and other environmental characteristics to be measured, and the frequency and manner of sampling are worked out between the discharger and EPA or a state agency. Many residuals are not specified in the permits.

Limitations of Permit Programs

There are, however, several shortcomings of the NPDES program. There is no quality control or certification program covering the laboratories submitting analytical reports. (See Chapter 3 for further discussion.) Inconsistencies exist in permit requirements for industries with the same SIC code. Important omissions in coverage have become evident. Since source monitoring by state and local environmental protection agencies is limited, there are too few techniques available to evaluate the self-monitoring by industry. It appears that some industries have failed to file permit applications. Few data seem to be available from NPDES permits on sludge production, storage, and disposal. Data collected are not stored in ways to make them useful for other purposes. In addition, because of statutory limitations, the portion of the NPDES program operated by EPA does not cover discharge of wastes to wells, although the 27 NPDES programs delegated to states do cover these discharges. EPA may be able to regulate such discharges, however, under the Safe Drinking Water Act.

Inadequacy for Identification and Forecasting of Industrial Wastes   No programs currently require industry to monitor the components of its manufacturing processes. Such monitoring would take account of the fact that industrial wastes are continually changing. Because sampling is not based on production schedules or tied to the components of processes, the cause of the discharge of harmful wastes frequently is not identified in time to prevent harm.

In many cases, industry is already capable of monitoring the components of its processes to detect changes from routine operations, and is therefore able to predict unusual types of residuals or increased levels of familiar ones. By altering operations or appropriately treating resultant wastes, industry could prevent environmental damage. Such practices should be fostered.

Substances Not Covered by Permit Programs The Toxic Substances Control Act of 1976 empowers EPA to regulate the manufacture, processing, and disposal of new chemicals; EPA may require industries to test these chemicals to determine their environmental effects. Harmful wastes, however, may be formed from industrial processes that are in no way related to the manufacturing or processing of new chemicals. These wastes may be toxic in themselves, or may combine with other residuals to form a toxic substance. Currently, industry is not required to assess the environmental effects of such wastes although many leading manufacturers do. EPA should encourage this practice.

• *We recommend to industry that, before a new product is manufactured or a new process instituted that may significantly affect environmental quality, it identify the substances that will be discharged and assess their potential environmental effects.*

EPA should provide guidance to industry in this area. Information on significant new effects should be made available to EPA and state environmental protection agencies. In addition, potentially harmful raw materials should be accompanied through each stage of their distribution by information on their relevant chemical and biological properties and by suggestions for their safe disposal.

TRANSPORTATION OF HAZARDOUS SUBSTANCES

Toxic and other hazardous substances are usually discovered to be present in the environment through special monitoring efforts only after a substance is discovered to be hazardous or after spills or discharges. If part of the manufacture, storage, transportation, distribution, and use of some chemicals were monitored, pollution could be anticipated. Efforts to prevent transportation accidents that cause pollution are inadequate.

The Department of Transportation, which regulates transportation of hazardous substances, has no effective program to prevent or minimize the danger of spills that affect water resources. The Federal Water Pollution Control Act of 1972 provides for EPA regulation of spills of oil and hazardous substances. Proposed regulations announced by EPA designated 306 hazardous substances and required notification concerning harmful quantities of substances entering the nation's waterways by any mode of transportation. Based on the results of monitoring the type, cause, frequency, and location of reported accidents involving release of any of the specific hazardous substances, EPA and the U.S. Coast Guard plan to develop regulations aimed at preventing such accidents or at least diminishing their effects. The Ports and Waterways Safety Act of 1972 (PL 92-340) gives the U.S. Coast Guard broad authority to control vessel traffic and related activities. The legislative history of this law shows that the "emphasis . . . is on new standards and regulations to prevent damage to the environment" (U.S. Congress, Senate 1972). The Hazardous Materials Transportation Act of 1975 requires shippers and manufacturers of containers used for hazardous substances to file a registration statement of compliance with prescribed safety standards with the Secretary of Commerce. The Resource Conservation and Recovery Act of 1976 gives EPA authority to regulate the transportation of hazardous wastes. Except for radioactive materials, however, no federal agency, however, has the authority to require carriers to report policies and plans for transporting other possibly hazardous substances. We do not suggest a routine reporting system, but this authority is needed so that such transport can be monitored when and where it poses a danger to the public. Some of the safeguards, policies, and procedures for transporting radioactive materials might be applied to the transport of other hazardous substances.

• *We recommend that EPA, other appropriate federal agencies, and carriers and shippers formulate guidelines and plans for the safe transport of hazardous substances. We also recommend that a federal agency be given the authority to require carriers to report such plans when deemed necessary.*

A carrier of chemicals is not even required to include the scientific name of a chemical on bills of lading. When a spill occurs, this information is needed to determine the degree of danger and the appropriate form of treatment. The Manufacturing Chemists Association provides some of this information over the telephone through their Chemical Transportation Emergency Center.

• *We recommend that bills of lading for possibly hazardous substances include the scientific name of chemicals being shipped.*

WASTEWATER TREATMENT

The number of wastewater treatment facilities has increased enormously because of federal and state laws and programs, including an $18 billion national construction program administered by EPA. The Agency estimates (U.S. EPA 1977) that another $150 billion may be needed to construct or improve sewers, and to upgrade treatment plants to provide secondary and tertiary treatment, in order to meet 1983 goals.[1]

In view of evidence[2] that many municipal wastewater treatment plants are not operating as designed, EPA should provide better monitoring procedures and technical assistance to evaluate the efficiency of such plants. When problems exist, studies should be made to determine whether they are due to overloading, technical management (operation, training, and manpower), or design. These diagnostic studies would enable EPA to improve the design and operation of treatment plants and to determine whether, in achieving water quality standards, it is more efficient to allocate some resources to municipal sewerage systems for operation and maintenance than for construction.

AMBIENT MONITORING

Efforts to improve EPA monitoring programs first require an unambiguous statement of objectives and criteria that are useful for the design and

---

[1]Primary treatment involves screening-out the floating solids in the water and then holding the water for a period of time to let other solids settle to the bottom of a tank.

Secondary treatment adds a biological process to primary treatment by allowing bacteria to consume some of the wastes in the water. Primary and secondary treatment remove some of the disease-carrying bacteria, and chlorination can be used after treatment to eliminate the remainder of such disease agents. But neither primary nor secondary treatment is very effective against the viruses and chemicals that currently represent some of the most important water-related health problems.

Tertiary treatment entails adding one or a series of biological or chemical removal processes to the physical and biological treatment stages. This treatment can remove most of the phosphorous components, thereby retarding or preventing eutrophication, and it can also remove a variety of other chemicals that wastewater may contain.

[2]In December 1976, the Comptroller General issued a report to Congress which contended that EPA was financing advanced waste treatment facilities without adequate water quality data or planning. It argued that both EPA and the states need to obtain better water quality information and to consider all water pollution control alternatives, in order to result in cost–effective treatment methods (U.S. GAO 1976a).

An indication of some common problems facing wastewater treatment plants may be obtained from a study of 20 treatment plants operated by the Department of Defense (U.S. GAO 1976b). In the survey, 18 treatment facilities were judged to be unsatisfactory under EPA criteria for rating plants. Overloading at 17 plants resulted in the discharge of effluent into receiving waters without adequate treatment. Chlorination facilities at 12 of the plants were inadequate with three plants lacking chlorine contact chambers and nine plants using inadequately designed chambers. The report also cited problems with inadequate sludge pumps, floating sludge in clarifiers, lack of flow meters on recirculating pumps, and unsuitable influent flow meters.

Another study we reviewed was on the monitoring of the influent of industrial wastes to treatment plants in Philadelphia (Slap 1976). The municipality is required to report information to EPA on residuals in the influent, but many residuals expected from some industries the plant serves were not reported.

evaluation of ambient monitoring networks. After networks are designed, prototypes and other techniques should be developed for efficiently putting them into operation.

Two important purposes of current ambient monitoring are to determine (a) how well environmental standards are being met (surveillance), and (b) how environmental quality is changing over time (trends). The determinations are important not only in administering pollution controls but also in evaluating the effectiveness of current environmental programs. Any such evaluation should compare current environmental quality with the quality that might be achieved if alternative strategies of pollution abatement were used.

SURVEILLANCE NETWORKS

Myriad data on the nation's environmental quality are collected from surveillance networks to detect violations or to confirm compliance with standards. Federal agencies alone account for about 9,000 monitoring stations for surface water quality and 3,000 for groundwater quality (USGS 1975); many more stations are operated by state and local governments. Most of these data find their way into STORET, the EPA ambient water quality data bank. Costs for monitoring ambient water quality have not been compiled systematically. The annual cost of EPA's ambient water monitoring is approximately $50 million, and it represents only a small portion of the national total.

Surveillance networks, which are designed to detect violations of standards of ambient environmental quality, often fail to provide other information important to environmental management. Because EPA examines most pollutant concentrations only to ascertain compliance with regulations, data are often of no use to determine mass balances, which are needed for the analysis and prediction of ambient air and water quality. Furthermore, in the case of water pollution, most of the data are collected in proximity to known discharges of pollutants with little apparent attention to the relationship between sampling times and hydrologic events. Where these data are not part of downstream profiles under known hydrologic conditions, such as rates of flow, one cannot calculate mass balances or relate ambient water quality to pollutant discharges.

Similar drawbacks with ambient air quality surveillance networks cause difficulties in relating ambient air quality to effects: stations are located in areas with high concentrations of pollutants, and little is known of the relationship between measurements from fixed stations and actual levels of human exposure.

Special surveys can provide information on the geographical distribution of pollutants that cannot be provided by a network of fixed stations. It seems essential, therefore, that EPA supplement a fixed-station network either with statistically controlled samples that are stratified according to different characteristics of water and air bodies, or with a cycle of intensive regional surveys that is repeated every few years. Moreover, selecting the location of a new fixed station should follow detailed sample surveys so that the location is sensitive to temporal, as well as spatial factors. In addition, the station should be located where there is a satisfactory accounting of pollutant sources. If a fixed station network is only to provide for sampling of the general quality of the monitored medium, without information to relate sources of pollution to ambient environmental quality, then this purpose might be more efficiently met by a national plan of stratified samples.

Actions based on faulty monitoring data from surveillance networks can have serious consequences. For example, stations in California's South Coast Air Basin have been reporting oxidant values with inaccuracies ranging from 10 percent low to 25 percent high for the past 9 to 19 years. On a single day in 1973, 8 of 16 cities either called health advisory alerts and emergencies incorrectly or reported violations of the air quality standards incorrectly as a result of poor data (Pitts et al. 1976). In Pittsburgh, failure to correct for water vapor interference in carbon monoxide measurements led to systematically high readings and more stringent transportation control measures than were desirable. (Requirements were established for air-bleed retrofits on pre-1968 model cars.) Similarly, some cities, because of poor data, may have failed to take necessary action.

Selecting Network Designs
on the Basis of Cost–Effectiveness

Many reports have been written concerning the design of water quality surveillance networks for efficiently detecting excessive concentrations of pollutants, but their results have not been practically applied. EPA's decisions concerning prediction and management of water quality are, for the most part, not based on data from these networks. Data from surveillance networks should be improved to serve additional purposes of environmental management.

We examined two recent EPA reports that recognize some of the differences among designs of ambient water quality monitoring programs and provide new guidance for them: *Model State Water Monitoring*

Program (U.S. EPA 1975a) and *Basic Water Monitoring Program* .[3] While incorporating several new techniques, they prescribe no indications of effectiveness; nor do they report or recommend tests or examinations to show whether the proposed networks will fulfill expectations in the years ahead. They lack analysis entirely. New networks are proposed to replace a current one without evident analysis of the existing network to justify the change, let alone to choose among alternatives. The idea for a new network apparently results from wide dissatisfaction with the evaluation of trends. Without a policy and a scientific basis for a proposed network, new networks may be discarded as quickly as those they were meant to replace.

The design of a surveillance network should determine location and number of monitoring stations and sampling frequency to detect violations either with a specified probability at minimum cost or with a maximum probability at a given cost. There is no simple way to assess economic benefits from the collection of data and, therefore, no simple way to gauge the optimum economic size of a program or to compare the effectiveness of data programs used by different groups for different purposes. A useful criterion for selecting network design, however, is cost–effectiveness. By this criterion, designs are chosen that either achieve a specified level of effectiveness for least cost, or maximum effectiveness for a specified cost. In either case, the trade-offs between cost and effectiveness should be analyzed.

In recent years, there have been a number of research reports, some published by EPA, to describe various methods for designing ambient water quality monitoring systems (Beckers et al. 1972, Ward 1973, Beckers and Chamberlain 1974, Crouch et al. 1976, Ward and Freeman 1973, Sherwani and Moreau 1975, Sanders et al. 1976). By revealing the costs related to errors of data and the consequences of incorrect inferences, these studies enable one to select a cost–effective design from various proposed schemes. The results of these studies, however, do not appear to be integrated into EPA's operations. They fail to demonstrate that users and operators of networks agree on criteria that are relevant to their needs. Because EPA did not supply the initial criteria for design, many of these reports differ in their techniques and fault the assumptions and criteria developed in the other reports. EPA might apply these diverse concepts of design to a common set of examples to determine how the various assumptions affect results and to judge which criteria and designs best serve the Agency's objectives.

[3]U.S. Environmental Protection Agency (1976) Basic Water Monitoring Program. Draft Report of the EPA Standing Work Group on Water Monitoring. (Internal Document)

Use of Prototypes   Prototype studies are needed to show how EPA, states, and others participating in a monitoring program can make decisions about the design of a cost–effective ambient network. The development of prototypes would call for, and may force, statements making clear how objectives and measures of effectiveness and other criteria for monitoring would actually function in practice. EPA should work with other federal agencies and the states to develop prototypes that demonstrate by example the analyses to be made of existing data. These prototypes should also show how alternative monitoring strategies can be improved to measure ambient quality and relate it to sources and effects of residuals. Given the complexity of the environment, it is not likely that a single monitoring strategy will be satisfactory for all places at all times. We propose rather that EPA avoid premature fixed commitments and invest in prototype examples and research to improve monitoring.

- *We recommend that EPA base its proposals and designs for ambient monitoring networks on prototype studies developed in cooperation with other federal agencies and the states.*

Research conducted by USGS on the Willamette River in Oregon (Hines et al. 1975, 1976; Jennings et al. 1976; Rickert and Hines 1975; Rickert et al. 1976a, 1976b, 1976c, 1977; Shearman 1976) is an example of the kind of work needed to develop prototypes that EPA might choose to employ, among others. These prototype studies should examine and incorporate a diversity of useful strategies and measures of effectiveness. The work could be carried out most effectively through the Office of Science (see Chapter 4).

The factors to be considered in the evolution of a prototype analysis are complex and will include consideration of the following:

1. The purposes of the data and how they are to be used for decisions and for research.

(a) Range of policy and research issues to be resolved and decisions to be made.

(b) Diversity of regions to be monitored.

(c) Types of environmental problems.

(d) Users of the data.

(e) Kinds of data needed (such as physical, meteorologic, hydrologic, or chemical data; or data on mass balances).

(f) Analyses to be made of the data for determining trends, detecting or forecasting violations of standards, and understanding relationships among sources of pollution, ambient environmental quality, and effects.

2. The statistical and engineering principles and criteria to be applied in the design and evaluation of monitoring networks.

(a) Kinds of models (e.g., mass balances, dynamic, kinematic, regression).

(b) Strategies for collection (fixed stations, spot sampling, intensive surveys of river segments, mobile sample surveys, continuous or intermittent sampling).

(c) Criteria for determining effectiveness of data plans (cost–effectiveness, tests to establish optimal frequency and numbers of observations, feedback from field tests).

(d) Dynamics of existing pollution sources, meteorology, and hydrology.

An example of clearly defined operational objectives can be seen in the design of USGS networks for monitoring water resources. The number of stations, the frequency of measurements, and the length of operation are evaluated often in order to facilitate making inferences from models (Moss and Karlinger 1974). In this way, an improved network evolves. The same principles should be applied to the design and development of air and water quality networks.

Retrospective Case Studies Because environmental problems are so complex that the extent of data and analysis necessary to resolve policy issues cannot be foreseen, we suggest that retrospective case studies should be conducted to provide detailed examinations of past monitoring programs in a particular region, and of the decisions based on such monitoring. This type of study would aid the development of cost–effective networks. As an example, our evaluation of the data networks in the Maumee "Estuary" (see Appendix B) provided insights with which to plan future monitoring more efficiently. The USGS study of the Willamette River (Hines et al. 1975, 1976; Jennings et al. 1976; Rickert and Hines 1975; Rickert et al. 1976a, 1976b, 1976c, 1977; Shearman 1976) also contains an analysis of data networks.

The Maumee study showed that different purposes for monitoring require different data. If the only purpose is to identify major problems or to trigger collection of data for enforcement proceedings, then data which are currently collected are acceptable. If the purpose is to model the estuary to predict effects of changes in types or amounts of pollutants discharged, then the current monitoring system is inadequate. A different plan is needed to help monitor and evaluate the performance of the water quality management:

Many of the relevant decisions can be drawn from long-term averages (for which acceptable results can often be drawn through mass balances deduced from a modest analytical framework) requiring no further data collection or modeling. Where water quality processes are under study, short-term intensive programs are indicated, to be repeated after several years. This suggests that the Maumee data program, as elsewhere, may be planned about a set of observations for mass balances, supplemented by periodic short-term intensive programs. (Maumee Estuary: A Case Study, Appendix B.)

After the problem and data needs are outlined, subsequent analysis can produce a more efficient plan for monitoring. Data planning can be a continual learning process only when there is systematic feedback from experience.

An evaluation of water quality requires concurrent information about the quantity and variation of flow. This need was also illustrated in our Maumee study. Ambient water quality networks should therefore be tied to appropriate hydrologic units, such as those of the Water Resources Council. Water is not constrained by political boundaries. Descriptions of the bed, bank, and appearances of other environs of the river, which so often represent the public's perception of pollution, should sometimes accompany the water quality data that are collected.

Some Types of Surveillance Monitoring

Land-use Inventories   Since patterns of land use help to determine ambient enviromental quality, data from maps and land-use inventories are valuable assets in understanding the potential environmental impact of new uses of land, in forecasting needs for pollution control by industries and municipalities, in anticipating needs for wastewater treatment plants, and in predicting where new pollution problems may arise as a result of increased urban, industrial, or agricultural development. These purposes could be served, but only in part, by the USGS Land Use and Land Cover Data and Analysis Program.

Remote Sensing   Remote sensing, especially from space satellites shows promise as a means of monitoring land use. Lasers mounted on aircraft have been used to detect and measure pollutants in both air and water. In Pittsburgh, a water pollution source inventory was checked by the EPA Environmental Monitoring and Support Laboratory, Las Vegas, through photographs taken from airplanes. Cooperative studies in 1972 by USGS and NASA, at the request of EPA, cited the complex chain of events that may lead to the pollution of groundwater by man's activities, and described some of the visible phenomena that can be observed by remote sensors as pollution indicators. Among the indicators are actual pollutants themselves (smoke, spills, effluents detectable by color differences or thermal effects), industries or activities that generate actual or potential pollutants, and surface cover types associated with particular pollutants.

Groundwater   It is important to note that groundwater, because of its widespread distribution and general purity, serves far more water supplies than do surface waters. Yet, because groundwater is a local resource, its problems are studied locally. Once groundwater is contaminated it may not cleanse itself for many years. Thus, the objective of monitoring groundwater should be the prevention of pollution. National technical leadership is needed if only because skills in groundwater hydrology are unevenly distributed.

Use of Models

EPA's surveillance networks could provide some of the data needed for designing models to relate source emissions to ambient environmental quality and to their ultimate effects. Data for this purpose are insufficient.

Models are tools for forecasting the results of environmental management and are useful in two important ways:

1. *To set and evaluate alternative control strategies.* Models can be used to help determine ambient standards and effluent guidelines, to allocate residual loadings, and to determine the effect of an alternative pollution control strategy on environmental quality.

2. *To determine the need for control.* Meteorological models predict pollution episodes; river basin models predict effects of new sources of pollution on water quality; and ecological models show trends in some effects.

The development of environmental models, in particular those that relate sources of pollution to ambient environmental quality, has been rapid. The need for data basic to the practical application of these models has outpaced their availability. If these models are to be applied, greater priority must be given to providing the data needed to develop and validate them.

TRENDS

Trends (changes over time) in environmental quality must be measured to keep watch for environmental problems, to evaluate pollution control programs, and to determine the need for further control. A network to determine trends should be designed so that the location and operation of stations to measure specified characteristics for a period of time are adequate to detect a change despite the patterns of variability in the data record.

Two national monitoring systems of fixed stations provide data on trends in water quality: the EPA National Water Quality Surveillance System (NWQSS), which the Agency plans to discontinue, and the National Stream Quality Accounting Network (NASQAN) of USGS. Both systems provide national coverage of ambient water quality, but such coverage does not mean they provide a synoptic national picture.

Because the national networks were inadequate to provide information on trends for many environmental characteristics, the Council on Environmental Quality (CEQ), in their Sixth Annual Report (CEQ 1976), used what data were available from the records in STORET (the EPA ambient water quality data bank) to determine the percentage of times ambient standards had been exceeded. The findings of the study may not be the result so much of changes in ambient water quality as of differences over time, and from place to place, in sample location, river flow, data collection methods, or laboratory procedures.

Determining Base Levels of Residuals

The measurement of trends requires a base from which to measure changes. This base is similar to a control group in a scientific experiment—both are used to provide a point of comparison and to eliminate, as far as possible, the effects of extraneous factors on the measurements. At present, there are not enough monitoring programs to establish a base from which to measure changes in levels or effects of residuals; thus, there are no accurate pictures of many important trends in environmental quality. Establishing a base is important for another purpose: before pollution control programs are planned or ambient standards set, it is desirable to know the pollution contribution from natural sources and natural transport, such as drainage from storms, windblown dust, and cosmic radiation. EPA needs to increase its attention to monitoring natural sources of environmental pollutants.

There are two ways to establish a base for the purpose of detecting changes in levels of residuals in an area. One is by monitoring in an area with hydrologic or meteorologic characteristics similar to the area being studied but possessing only minor sources of man-made pollution. Another is by monitoring in a consistent manner before and after new sources of environmental degradation occur or new control programs are established. It is also possible to combine the two methods just described to be able to compare series. Whatever method is used some monitoring will be required where there are relatively few pollution problems.

Although most monitoring is conducted in areas with pollution problems, three programs exist for establishing bases. Two of these were established because future sources of pollution were evident and the need for obtaining data before the predicted pollution occurred was recognized. One is an effort to provide base levels of pollutants in nine western states in which energy resources, such as low-sulfur coal, oil shale, uranium deposits, and oil and gas formations, are to be explored and in which coal-fired power plants will be built. This effort involves 17 federal agencies and is coordinated by EPA. The other is a Bureau of Land Management program to study the outer continental shelf in areas where off-shore oil drilling is planned. The third program is under the direction of USGS. It is designed to establish a base in water quantity and quality by monitoring in 57 hydrologic bench marks, sites that are presumed to be nearly natural in condition and will remain significantly unchanged by man (Cobb and Biesecker 1971).

In some programs, the need for a control group has led to monitoring in areas with few or no serious pollution problems. For example, the EPA Community Health and Environmental Surveillance Study (CHESS) purposely chose areas with both high and low concentrations of common air pollutants. In the EPA National Water Quality Surveillance System (NWQSS), pairs of stations were established upstream and downstream of areas with sources of pollution, and areas with different patterns of land use were selected.

The two methods of establishing a base—monitoring in different areas or monitoring at different times—both require measurement procedures capable of being compared. When inconsistent measurements are taken, observed changes in environmental quality could be the result of the different sampling and measurement methods themselves. Many air quality measurement methods have changed as inaccuracies were discovered (Kinosian 1977). Attention is needed to the calibration of methods against one another. Moreover, sampling and measurement methods for both air and water pollutants differ among agencies, and there is large variability among results obtained from different analytical laboratories. We discuss these problems of the measurement process in Chapter 3.

The Office of Science in EPA that we propose (see Chapter 4) could provide the scientific leadership to co-ordinate measurement activities and policies for monitoring the environment in areas untroubled by pollution.

New Programs Needed to Determine Bases

Inventories of Substances The discovery of the harmful effects of mercury and PCB led to questions concerning their occurrence in the environment. Although the sources and ambient levels of a number of common pollutants are monitored, knowledge of many other residuals that may be equally important to human health and environmental quality is far from complete. Base levels for many residuals could be established, ideally, with a quantitative assessment now of parts of the environment that could be scrutinized years later to detect the presence of chemicals that proved to have adverse effects. With modern techniques, such as gas chromatography and mass spectrometry, one can now measure small quantities and analyze many general characteristics of chemicals in samples of air, water, soil, and biota. Information from gas chromatograms and mass spectrograms could be obtained and saved for future reference. When a harmful effect of a chemical is discovered, the records could be analyzed to determine when, where, and in what amounts the chemical was present in the environment. This procedure would allow a rapid assessment of the magnitude of an environmental problem.

- *We recommend that EPA analyze samples of the environment for the presence and quantity of selected chemicals. Samples of air, water, soil, and biota should be periodically collected from carefully selected sites in different parts of the country, and analyzed. Gas chromatograms and mass spectrograms should be preserved for retrospective analysis of chemicals later recognized to have adverse effects.*

We suggest that one to three laboratories be equipped and charged with this task as their primary responsibility. Samples cannot be analyzed for all chemicals; efforts should first be directed at identifying those, such as pesticides, that are suspected of having adverse effects on health or the ecology. Some EPA laboratories currently save some analytical records of their analyses.

Acid Precipitation Program The quality of precipitation has signficant ecological effects. For example, acid precipitation with a pH of less than 4.0 can leach nutrients from soils, which over the long-term could result in decreased growth of vegetation, particularly forests. There is evidence that acid precipitation has been increasing in some areas, that it reduces the abundance and diversity of fish and micro-flora and fauna of rivers and lakes, and that it increases corrosion of materials. It is particularly a problem in those areas, such as the eastern United States, where quantities of sulfur and nitrogen oxides that occur by emission and transport are larger than in other areas (NRC 1975). The problems created by acid precipitation have been recognized for more than eight years. There is at present no national network for monitoring the acidity of rainwater and particulates that fall to the earth, although one is being planned by the U.S. Department of Agriculture in cooperation with other federal agencies. The USGS Office of Water Data Coordination through its Federal Advisory Committee is reviewing federal programs in this area with the objective of preparing recommendations for an observational network. EPA analyzes precipitation sampled by NOAA at 20 locations, most of which are in the Northeast. Central leadership is needed to coordinate and make compatible the few efforts that are being made to monitor such acidity and its effects.

• *We recommend the establishment, following prototype studies, of a national network to monitor the acidity and other characteristics of precipitation and particulates that fall to the earth.*

EPA should either study or support studies of the ecological and other effects of this acidity and the effects of other pollutants carried by precipitation.

HEALTH EFFECTS MONITORING AND EPIDEMIOLOGY

The costs of air pollution control can be estimated, albeit with difficulty and uncertainty. The health benefits of control are far more difficult to quantify, and many are unknown. They cannot be determined by toxicological studies, which face the problem of extrapolation from animals to man, or by clinical studies, which are unable to duplicate long-term chronic conditions. Only through long-term epidemiological studies can one hope to solve the problem.

PROBLEMS WITH FEDERAL AIR POLLUTION EPIDEMIOLOGY

CHESS was the largest epidemiological effort ever mounted to relate air pollution to human health. The program however, was fraught with scientific problems and led to questionable results. It was ended in mid-1975. As a pioneering effort, CHESS labored under extraordinary hardships, including inadequate air pollution measurement technology, inadequate historical data on air quality, and an inability to measure the actual exposure of individuals. Nonetheless, one of its major findings—

the identification of sulfates as an important health problem—remains generally accepted.

Other findings in EPA's only major published report on CHESS (U.S. EPA 1974) have come under serious attack.[4] Two major reviews of these findings (U.S. EPA 1975b, Dillaway and Byerly 1976) revealed that gross errors in the measurement of pollutant concentrations were common. Concentrations were extrapolated on the basis of a single year's data from a single station, although additional data were available from nearby stations for other years; and estimates of "threshold" concentrations of pollutants, below which no harm to human health is assumed, were given without an indication of the possible range of uncertainty. These problems with statistical and measurement practices were serious enough to invalidate the quantitative dose-response relationships, which were one goal of the study. A wider scientific review of the initial design of the CHESS studies and of its major report (U.S. EPA 1974) would have resulted in a more valuable contribution to the nation's air quality control strategies. (In Chapter 4, we suggest that the Office of Science provide for such reviews.)

Although solutions have been found for some of the problems confronted by CHESS, new air pollution epidemiological studies still face serious difficulties. For example, if a single pollutant accounts for a substantial share of the health effects of air pollution, but has not yet been recognized as harmful and hence is not measured during the study, the results may be affected. Another difficulty is that, because levels of many pollutants are highly correlated, their separate contributions may not be clearly determined. Some other difficulties are that many environmental measurement methods are of questionable accuracy; there are many possible pollutants and many possible health effects to measure; there is much variability among responses of individuals; and people differ in their patterns of exposure to air pollution within a community and from one community to another.

Measuring Particulate Matter

The current method for measuring particulate matter is inadequate to meet the needs of air pollution epidemiology studies. Not all types of particulate matter cause the same harm to man; particles larger than a few microns are not likely to travel beyond the upper respiratory airways and be deposited deeply in the lungs. It is not clear as to whether particles

[4]See the paper by L. Wallace, "The CHESS story: a summary of major reviews" (working paper prepared for the NRC Study Group on Environmental Monitoring, [1977]: Appendix F describes the availability of this manuscript).

smaller than a tenth of a micron are harmful, but there is evidence that such particles are deposited and retained in the lung. The current method for measuring particulate matter by mass gives undue weight to the larger particles. It accepts all particles up to 100 microns in diameter; yet a 100-micron particle has a million times the mass of a 1-micron particle. Information about the mass of particles 0.1 to 3.5 microns in diameter, which are of respirable size, would be more useful to determine health effects. Also useful would be information on the size distribution, chemical composition, and shape of the respirable particles.

There are problems with the filters used in the measurement method for particles. Impurities in glass fiber filters adversely affect analytical measures for sulfates and nitrates. The development of a single filter that would allow determination of these substances and of respirable particle concentrations would be desirable. Another problem with these filters is that, by their allowing conversion of sulfur dioxide to sulfate, they cause erroneously high sulfate measurements. This problem adversely affected measurements used in CHESS and was a factor in the questions raised about the validity of its conclusions.

EPA has contributed to the development and use of several types of air samplers that can divide atmospheric particles into two or more size ranges. Two types of dichotomous samplers have been developed and tested: a virtual impactor, which allows particles to pass through a neck into a chamber where they are separated by an angled stream of air, and a system of two filters with different diameters in series. The virtual impactor has the advantage of eliminating particle bounce, which reduces the collection efficiency of conventional impactors. Agencies in Nevada and Texas have also done studies to monitor for respirable size particulates.

- *We recommend that EPA sponsor further development of equipment to measure the respirable fraction of particulate matter. We also recommend that stations in the National Aerometric Data Bank move toward further measuring and reporting of the mass of both the respirable fraction and total of suspended particulate matter.*

It may only be necessary to conduct periodic surveys to determine the respirable fraction of airborne particulate matter and its relation to other measurements, rather than to equip each station to measure it continually.

Determining Chemical Composition of Particulates

The health effects of airborne particles are determined not only by their size but also by their chemical composition. For example, animal studies have shown differences in the toxicity of different kinds of sulfates (Amdur 1977). A rapid and relatively inexpensive way to determine chemical composition is needed. At least one method, X-ray fluorescence spectroscopy, shows promise of fulfilling these requirements. The relative amounts of most elements with atomic numbers above 12 can be determined in a few minutes without the need for special sample preparation and at reasonable cost. The method was tested in conjunction with a dichotomous sampler by EPA in 1973, and was successful in determining differences in chemical composition between the respirable and nonrespirable parts of total suspended particulates (Dzubay and Stevens 1973). Periodic surveys in a locality may suffice to determine the chemical composition of particulates there.

Measuring Actual Human Exposure

An additional problem for epidemiological studies is that data collected from fixed stations in an ambient monitoring network may poorly represent the true concentrations to which the human population is exposed. The ultimate ambient sampler of materials to which man is exposed is man himself. Measurements of actual human exposure to pollutants would provide important data to study the effects of various levels of pollutants on humans, animals, and plants, and would help to determine effects of geographic and temporal differences of ambient air quality.

EPA is currently trying to strengthen its program of monitoring human exposure. The Agency has been using mobile vans for urban sampling and is further considering methods for measuring the indoor concentrations of pollutants and the development of human activity models for predicting total exposure based on time spent indoors, commuting, and working.

A serious gap in this otherwise commendable activity is that the Agency is not currently developing personal air quality monitors. Information from these monitors would serve to calibrate the data from networks of fixed stations for studies of the effects of air pollution and for environmental management decisions. By equipping a controlled sample of people with these portable sampling devices, the concentration of air pollutants to which they are exposed could be measured. This information would permit calibration and validation of exposures estimated with models that use other measurements. There is evidence to challenge a common objection that personal monitors are technologically impractical (Harrison et al. 1976, Morgan and Morris 1976, Wallace 1977). Prototypes have recently been developed to detect several air pollutants at levels near ambient concentrations (Wallace 1977). Because demand for such an item may be too small to provide adequate profits, industry may require financial support to undertake the necessary research and development.

* *We recommend that EPA coordinate and support a program to foster the development of small, quiet, sensitive, and accurate personal air pollution monitors for use in conjunction with other methods of measuring human exposure to ambient air quality.*

In implementing this recommendation, EPA should rely on the extensive experience of NIOSH, ERDA, and the Bureau of Mines. In addition, industries, universities, and federal laboratories with experience in technical development of air quality measurement equipment should be involved.

COORDINATION OF A NEW EPIDEMIOLOGY PROGRAM

With improved knowledge of the chemical and physical nature of pollutants and the actual concentrations to which humans are exposed, better large-scale epidemiological studies can be planned. Such studies are essential for sound air quality management. Clearly, only federal government agencies have the resources and the mandate for supporting such studies in the United States.

Because of the magnitude and complexity of such an enterprise, the technological and environmental measurement expertise of the "environmental" agencies (EPA, NOAA, USGS) may have to be combined with the medical and epidemiological expertise of the "health" agencies (NCHS, NIH, NIOSH, OSHA). The National Institute of Environmental Health Sciences, for example, sponsors research in air pollution epidemiology, including one study of the health effects of air pollution in six cities that is conducted by a group at Harvard University (Speizer et al. 1977). We believe that although EPA may conduct special epidemiological studies, responsibility for long-term epidemiology should be shared among the agencies.

- *We recommend that careful planning begin immediately among various agencies most involved for a long-term, multi-city study of the effects of air pollution on human health, including both chronic and acute diseases.*

The study should include the effects of drinking water quality, where it is relevant in the etiology of the diseases studied. The water should be measured at the tap, not merely at mains or treatment plants. Planning should be coordinated by an interagency task force. (In Chapter 4, we suggest ways to coordinate federal environmental monitoring efforts.) Leading epidemiologists should be sought to take part in the effort. Pilot programs to test different health questionnaires, response rates, costs, and quality assurance should precede the full-scale study.

SURVEILLANCE OF HUMAN POPULATIONS

The growing conviction that chemicals in the environment are a major cause of cancer in humans is based on two types of evidence. One type is the observed relationship between the occurrence of specific tumors and occupational or personal exposure to particular chemicals. For example, there is a greater incidence of lung cancer in workers using asbestos and of bladder cancer in workers using coal tar or pitch than in the general population (Cole and Goldman 1975). Observed differences in the incidence of or mortality from specific tumors among a number of identifiable populations provide the second type of evidence. Studies comparing U.S. natives with emigrants from various countries show that, in an emigrant's lifetime, risks of cancer of the large bowel, breast, ovary, corpus uteri, and prostate rise to the prevailing level for the U.S. population (Haenszel 1975). Such differences may represent differences in exposure to some unidentified substances.

The discovery that an increased risk of cancer or other disease is associated with an occupational or personal exposure has depended on the astuteness of the physician. He either notices an apparent increase in the number of common tumors (such as those of the lung or bladder) or the unusual clustering of cases of an otherwise rare tumor (such as mesothelioma, associated with exposure to asbestos fibers, or angiosarcoma of the liver, associated with exposure to vinyl chloride). Such observations have later been confirmed by larger epidemiological studies, by the identification of possible offending agents, and by induction of a tumor in an experimental animal through exposure to the suspected agent. The identification of carcinogens has usually been based on relatively high exposures in well-defined population groups, such as cigarette smokers, workers using vinyl chloride, and menopausal women receiving estrogens. Can this process of discovery of new environmental risks by observation, epidemiology, and experimentation be broadened and enhanced by monitoring? We considered several ways to institutionalize this process.

Disease Detection

A disease detection program should be established based on continuing surveillance of particular groups of people who are or who have been exposed to chemicals known to be animal carcinogens but not yet identified as human carcinogens. The groups to be surveyed should consist of those people whose occupations expose them to high levels of animal carcinogens, and those who have had great exposure to widely distributed potential hazards such as pesticides. Exposure may sometimes be defined by measurements of body burden, the level of a substance within the body.

This method of measurement depends on the nature of the residual, how it is metabolized, and how it passes through the body. There are three types of materials that can be sampled in man: (1) acute poisons, for which analyses of expired air, blood, and urine are usually performed; (2) materials with relatively short biological half-lives that establish equilibrium levels under conditions of constant or recurrent exposure, such as carbon monoxide; and (3) materials with long biological half-lives that are stored and may be selectively concentrated. Important pollutants that are rapidly metabolized do not lend themselves to such body-burden determinations, because they do not accumulate. These pollutants include polycyclic hydrocarbons and sulfur oxides, which have cumulative effects over long periods of exposure. Identification of surrogate materials that do accumulate would serve to circumvent this difficulty. For example, it has been claimed that the body-burden of cadmium is an indicator of "cigarette-pack-years" of smoking.

Formidable problems attend the recruitment of a voluntary population from whom to draw samples, the establishment of standard protocols and compatibility of techniques for sampling and measurement, and the preservation of body tissue and fluids.

Monitoring systems for body burdens can be used to evaluate levels of exposure, to study the relationships between states of diseases and body burden, and to identify changes in body burden of pollutants. In addition, the preservation of tissues and fluids would permit retrospective assessment of pollutants.

Need for a National Death Index

Surveillance of large population groups for the effect of chemicals in air, water, and food can only be done by accurate case reporting and central indexing. Mortality statistics based on death certificates are inadequate indicators of cancer occurrence because of variations in diagnosis. If malignant tumors were a reportable disease in all jurisdictions, diagnosis would not be subject to uncertainty, because clinical diagnosis of cancer based on an examination of tissue would be required. The pathological basis for diagnosis could be included in the documentation of every reported case. In addition, history of residence, occupation, drug use, and other personal and social data could be included.

Such reporting, although ideal, is impractical as a nationwide program. There are already a few population-based cancer registers in the United States, and the National Cancer Institute (NCI) SEER program covers 10 percent of the U.S. population. A program with the necessary quality control to cover the entire population would be too costly. At present, research on the effects of suspected carcinogens must depend primarily on special retrospective studies. Studies to discover human carcinogens require hypothesizing that can only be done by experienced cancer epidemiologists.

Differences in morbidity and mortality among different populations, and increases in some types of disease lead us to suspect environmental causes. In cases where there is clinical and experimental evidence to implicate a particular agent (such as ultraviolet radiation as a cause of skin cancer), morbidity and mortality statistics are also useful in studying the relationships between levels of exposure and risks of contracting the disease.

The National Center for Health Statistics (NCHS) collects data on the nation's health. Improvement of its programs could provide better data for signaling possible effects of unidentified environmental hazards, for raising or allaying suspicions about particular chemicals in the environment, and for providing information on how a known environmental hazard causes harm to man. The Center should resume surveys that provide regional estimates of morbidity and special follow-up studies on diseases for which environmental agents are a suspected cause.

Those epidemiological studies of the health effects of environmental hazards that follow subjects until their death are often impeded by difficulties in obtaining the fact, cause, and time of death. Currently, many states must be searched for each death. Moreover, without the registration number of the death certificate, state vital statistics offices can only provide information about an individual death if they are given the approximate date of death and the identification of the person. With a national death index, a computerized alphabetical national listing of deaths by year of death, a researcher could determine which individuals in a list of study subjects died during a given year. Additional information in the index would enable the researcher to request a copy of the death certificate from the appropriate state vital statistics office and to follow up on related information.

> • *We recommend that the National Center for Health Statistics establish and operate a National Death Index. The index should provide the place of death, date of death, and state registration number of the death certificate.*

The index, because it would facilitate access to death certificates, may compromise individual privacy, but it would make more accessible only part of the information that would otherwise be available. Access could be limited to medical researchers. Easier accessibility to death certificates will increase their use, perhaps offsetting lost revenues to the states that are the only current source of information to confirm deaths.

Occupational Health Statistics

It is often thought that occupational health statistics promise early detection of environmental dangers. Most pollutants that impair health are first discovered in the industrial environment, where exposure is most intense and identification less complicated by the presence of other pollutants. Yet, even in the most publicized cases (DDT, vinyl chloride, asbestos, and PCB), conclusive evidence of damage to the general population (other than the relatives of workers) has yet to be established. The general population may not be affected by the lower dosages normally encountered in the environment, because the body may tolerate these dosages. If effects do exist, however, they may be difficult to detect. There may be long periods between exposure and the appearance of disease, or an effect may be obscured by its natural variability in the general population and by other factors that produce the same effect.

Because of public concern over the large number of chemicals introduced into the environment and the possibly harmful effects of some of them, chemicals can be regulated before they are manufactured. Under the Toxic Substances Control Act of 1976, EPA may require manufacturers to provide evidence of the safety of chemicals, new or old, that are suspected to be harmful. A well-designed system of occupational health statistics may identify some chemicals that demand further scrutiny.

Such a system might use records from many sources such as industry, unions, the Department of Agriculture, the Bureau of the Census, Bureau of Labor Statistics (BLS), EPA, Internal Revenue Service, NCI, NCHS, Occupational Safety and Health Administration (OSHA), and Social Security Administration to relate industrial or agricultural exposures to incidence of disease. Current statistics on occupational illness are collected by BLS under an agreement with OSHA.

The OSHA/BLS annual "Survey of Occupational Injuries and Illness" is not, however, adequate to determine incidence rates, relate exposures to illness, or identify harmful substances or hazardous industries. First, only obvious and acute reactions are recorded. The data do not provide for an assessment of chronic, long-term effects. Second, the categories of occupational disease developed by OSHA and BLS are confusing and not adequately informative. Illnesses are aggregated into coarse categories, and 20 to 25 percent of all diseases reported are categorized as "Other." Third, statistics on exposure data and causal agents are not collected, although the law requires employers to record such data for certain substances. Fourth, only numbers of cases, not incidence rates, are reported. A reported increase in the number of cases of a disease in a particular industry may only be the result of a larger number of workers in the industry. Suitable estimates of the working population by detail of occupation and type of exposure are lacking. So, for example, the incidence rate of an illness of workers exposed to a particular pollutant may not be determined. Finally, illnesses not yet known to have occupational causes can hardly be reported as occupational.

We suggest a number of ways to improve current occupational health statistics, but we are not sure that routine company reporting can be turned into an adequate instrument for discovering environmental hazards to the general population or for determining relationships between exposure to chemicals and illness. One improvement would be for BLS and OSHA to use a better classification of occupational illnesses. Here, the experienced specialists in industrial hygiene and epidemiology, and of Departments of Health of states and foreign countries (especially Scandinavian countries and England) could be consulted. Pilot programs to test whether definitions are clearly understood by employers and company doctors should precede the general use of definitions.

OSHA and other agencies should explore ways to improve the reporting and collection of data on the exposure of employees to chemicals. Some states have systems of occupational health statistics based on doctors' reports for workmen's compensation that often include some exposure data or suspected causal agents. Annual lists of suspected causal agents can identify chemicals on which to focus attention and may provide early warning of new dangers.

Available data should be analyzed to relate exposure to chemicals in the workplace to morbidity and mortality rates for workers in various geographic regions. These analyses would suggest associations that could be further evaluated by special studies.

A third step would be to improve estimates of the working population in different industries, so that incidence rates could be obtained, and to identify illnesses of the same worker, so that they would not be counted as new cases. When only the number of cases is available, important relationships might not be detected.

Special studies to collect occupational health statistics often provide more specific and more accurate data than can be obtained from improvements in routine record keeping. For this reason, they should be used to supplement information derived from records. A study by the National Institute for Occupational Safety and Health (Discher et al. 1975) involved visits to plants, medical examinations of workers and determination of exposures of workers with possible occupational disorders to noise and certain chemicals. The study found that less than 5 percent of the probable cases of occupational diseases it had identified were reported in either the OSHA/BLS survey or in records of state workmen's compensation claims.

The difference in the way occupations are classified in the census and on death certificates presents problems for occupational mortality studies. The current occupation of an individual is recorded in the decennial U.S. census of population, but the usual occupation during the person's lifetime is recorded on the death certificate. These two sets of data for 1950 were used to calculate age-specific occupational mortality rates and standardized mortality ratios of persons 25 to 68 years of age for different occupations. These rates were regarded as having limited value because of the difference in definition and the tendency to upgrade the status of occupations in reporting on decedents. Occupational mortality rates and ratios are established with greater care in other countries.

• *We recommend that the National Center for Health Statistics, the Bureau of the Census, and the National Institute for Occupational Safety and Health explore the completeness, specificity, and comparability of data on occupations reported in the census and on death certificates and, if warranted by the results, make plans for the coding of occupational data and calculation of appropriate measures of occupational mortality for the three-year period centered on the 1980 decennial census.*

Other Sources of Information
on Occupational Diseases

Because of the problems with current occupational health statistics, interest has increased in other sources of information to improve study and surveillance of occupational diseases. Upon closer scrutiny, the records that come to mind are found to be limited in their usefulness for these purposes. Employees' work records are the most useful.

Physicians' Records   Records kept by physicians at offices, clinics, or hospitals are of limited value in determining occupational diseases for several reasons. First, physicians may not recognize the occupational connection. Few medical schools have courses in industrial hygiene, so many physicians do not know what to suspect. Moreover, the cases may be widely separated in time and spread over many physicians, so that clusters are not noticed. Second, the worker may not recognize the occupational connection. Few efforts are made to educate the worker about occupational diseases. Third, physicians' records are not uniform with regard to definitions, information included, or methods of reporting occupation.

Workmen's Compensation Claims   Although compensation claims are a primary source of information about occupational disease, they also present problems. Coverage of workers and requirements for reporting vary from state to state under different workmen's compensation laws. (The National Commission on State Workmen's Compensation Laws recommended that all states be meeting certain basic requirements for coverage in 1975.) In addition, the claims tend to record only acute conditions with evident causes; chronic conditions that may be caused by exposure to chemicals in the workplace are not likely to be reported.

Social Security Disability Insurance   The Social Security Administration has records of persons no longer in the labor force because of disabling conditions, but the records do not include complete job histories and data on occupational exposure.

Employers' Records   Records of employers are of three types: (1) records on illness and injury required by the Occupational Safety and Health Act; (2) medical records kept by the company medical unit; and (3) all nonmedical records, such as payroll information. Unexpectedly, it is the third type that may have most value in studying occupational illness. The weaknesses in the records required by OSHA have been discussed, and serious problems of liability and invasion of individual privacy exist in the case of company medical records.

Payroll records are usually so detailed that individual workers can be identified and followed through changes of jobs in a complete work history. The records may also be retained for lengthy periods. These characteristics make such records possibly the only source of detailed information on the worker's history of exposure to industrial chemicals. Ways to insure the availability of such personnel records to qualified researchers need to be explored. The value of these records should be brought to the attention of employers who should be encouraged where feasible not to destroy them until sufficient time has elapsed to allow for possible effects from exposures. For some diseases, the period of time between exposure and appearance of the disease may be very long (for instance, for cancer of the bladder, anywhere from 2 to 45 years or longer [Case et al. 1954]). For other diseases, and even for cancer, the period can be considerably shorter.

● *We recommend to employers that where there is any signficant possibility of usefulness, they retain employees' work records, if feasible, for a length of time sufficient to permit epidemiological studies of occupational diseases.*

We suggest that OSHA provide guidance to industry on record retention.

Record Linkage

Record linkage refers to the merging of different records relating to the same individual. Sufficient linkage could allow epidemiologists to follow the occupational, residential, and medical history of a person throughout his life. This knowledge is particularly valuable because of the long latent periods associated with some diseases caused by environmental pollutants.

A number of countries with national health programs have adopted regional or national medical record linkage. Some conduct studies on occupational and environmental health effects that would not be possible without record linkage. In England, many studies have been made from the Oxford Record Linkage Study, which began in 1962. In Norway and Sweden, occupational mortality is studied by linking death certificates with occupational and residential data from a census. Denmark and Finland are performing similar studies. Sweden publishes morbidity statistics from a record linkage system of hospital discharges. Canada has a file of occupational histories taken from a 5 percent sample of the labor force that can be linked to death certificates and to a proposed National Cancer Register. It is thus possible to continuously monitor Canadian industry for adverse effects of industrial environments, no matter how long the effects may be delayed.

A few well-established systems of medical record linkage exist in the United States. The National Research Council's Medical Follow-up Agency has developed and applied methods for linking medical records of servicemen with records of the Veterans Administration. The records, however, have limited usefulness in determining environmental contributants to chronic disease: apart from residence history, information on the environmental exposure of veterans is generally limited to a few years of military service. The Mayo Clinic operates a centralized diagnostic registry for data on the medical care of all residents of Olmsted County, Minnesota. Although it is a source of more complete and integrated life-long medical records, its usefulness is limited by the small size and mobility of the population. Several population-based cancer registries, by linking diagnoses for the same individual, can report incidence rates based on the first diagnosis of a type of cancer and not merely on number of cases diagnosed.

These examples suggest that some type of national medical record linkage system may be both practicable and useful in the United States, but several problems must be overcome before it can be instituted. One problem is how to identify records of the same individual. Two people may have the same name, or people may change their names; addresses and occupations change. Social Security numbers have drawbacks: they are often forgotten or written incorrectly; many people have none; and some have more than one. Alternative approaches could make use of identifiers based on easily remembered personal information with extra information to help detect errors.

Another problem is the violation of the privacy of citizens. Many techniques have recently evolved for protecting confidentiality while maintaining access to records for research purposes, among them, the use of "alias" identifiers, or neutral "brokerage" agencies (Campbell et al. 1975, Boruch and Cecil 1977).

These and related problems must be weighed against the ultimate benefits of improved health. In addition to its usefulness in medical and health studies (NCHS 1968), record linkage could help to identify possible cause-effect relationships for chronic low-level exposures to current and potential pollutants and could help to identify environmental hazards in the workplace. Another advantage would be statistics based on the person, rather than the event.

• *We recommend that an interagency task force study issues of medical record linkage and weigh its benefits in increased knowledge of causes and extent of disease against its monetary and social costs, including invasions of privacy.*

Monitoring Human Genetic Effects

A promising activity of monitoring for discovery is surveillance to detect changes in human mutation rates. Findings of no increase in mutation rates would provide reassurance, but only if monitoring programs were designed in such a way that substantial changes in mutation rates were reasonably sure to be detected. Findings of increased mutation rates would provide evidence for the regulation of man-made mutagens and might need to be followed by studies to determine causal agents. Monitoring for human genetic effects is now technically feasible, but many important scientific and social problems remain to be studied. Among them are (a) analysis of the benefits to be obtained from early detection of large increases in mutation rates; (b) the statistical, economic, and technical feasibility of different types of designs; and (c) considerations of privacy, confidentiality, and informed consent. Methods that should be explored are the monitoring of population characteristics (stillbirth frequency, birthweight, congenital defects), sentinel phenotypes (Marfan's syndrome, retinoblastoma), and biochemical or chromosomal mutations (blood protein studies). In addition, research is needed on applications of the information obtained from such monitoring. Retrospective case-controlled studies may be needed to determine causal agents.

• *We recommend that the National Institutes of Health, the National Science Foundation, or another federal agency sponsor research policy conferences to discuss the scientific and social problems of monitoring for human genetic effects and the statistical, economic, and technical feasibility of various monitoring systems.*

Further scientific considerations for such monitoring are discussed in Appendix A.

ECOLOGICAL EFFECTS MONITORING

Surveillance of animals and plants provides a means for discovering the degree to which low-level chronic exposures to residuals affect ecological well-being and potentially affect humans. Research has shown the feasibility of using certain species of plants, animals, and microorganisms to monitor the environment. In some cases, this type of monitoring may be the best way to determine the synergistic impact of a combination of pollutants.

Monitoring for discovery of ecological effects depends in part on the development and use of indicator species, biota that are known to indicate changes in environmental quality by responses or by accumulation of residuals. For example, common plants such as tobacco or white pine can be used to provide low-cost networks sensitive to specific air pollutants. A Utah agency monitors indicator plants sensitive to hydrogen fluoride, sulfur dioxide, and ozone at over 100 locations in the state. A Tennessee agency monitors fluoride content in vegetation near fertilizer plants. A South Dakota agency monitors fish for the presence of mercury in rivers containing tailings from mining operations. No one animal or organism can serve as a universal pollutant indicator; the complexity of pollutant problems requires a diversity of indicators.

Ecological effects monitoring should also provide information on more direct consequences of environmental pollution for man. For example, data from such programs could indicate whether pollutants were affecting the economic value of crops. At present, the national secondary ambient air quality standard for sulfur dioxide (0.5 ppm for a three-hour average) is based on data on foliar injury and not on the growth and yield of plants.

EPA should coordinate and support research to develop accurate quantitative measures of responses of biota to changes in environmental quality for use in providing rapid warnings of the presence of contaminants, in determining changes in the levels of ecological effects, and in making predictions with models.

Relatively unexplored is the use of microbiological indicators in environmental monitoring. Some microorganisms, such as those that photosynthesize and provide the base of the food web for aquatic life, can provide a highly sensitive warning of environmental deterioration. Others, by changes in growth rates, can indicate changes in pollutant concentrations that are undetectable by chemical means. Microorganisms are particularly useful because of the ease in detecting them and the speed with which their populations grow. Of special value for exploration are the microbiological indicators for heavy metals, oil, and pesticides. For example, an increase in the number of microorganisms that are resistant to heavy metals gives information about the effects of dumping sludges or dredge spoils, and an increase in microorganisms that degrade petroleum gives information about effects of oil spills.

Hazardous consequences to man may result from pollution that first affects microorganisms. When sewage and heavy metals that occur in sludge from wastewater treatment plants are dumped into a body of water, changes in bacterial populations result. Selection of bacteria that are resistant to heavy metals can occur, and such bacteria are often resistant to antibiotics (Morgan et al. 1976). Thus there may be an enhancement of the growth of strains of bacteria that pose a potential problem to human health.

Biological effects monitoring is used more frequently in relation to water quality than to air quality. Initial results from a national inventory of biological monitoring programs, compiled by the Oak Ridge National Laboratory for the Council on Environmental Quality (see Appendix D), show 1017 programs that included biological monitoring of water quality as opposed to 35 for air quality.

An advantage of biological monitors is that they respond to many pollutants and not just those that are known. Chemical monitoring requires prior designation of the pollutant to be monitored. Biological monitoring, particularly with the use of microbiological indicators, can thus provide early warning of pollution problems.

We showed that special surveys should supplement monitoring stations to determine ambient air and water quality. The same conclusion applies to ecological effects. The National Eutrophication Survey employed sampling that was too scattered and too infrequent to monitor the critical pathways through which pollutants are transported. To determine the ecological effects of changes in ambient environmental quality, EPA should intensively monitor some entire ecosystems (e.g., an estuary or watershed) in problem areas.

EPA should lead in establishing a long-term ecological monitoring program and provide scientific goals and monitoring criteria.

- *We recommend that EPA coordinate and support long-term monitoring of natural, managed, and damaged ecosystems to identify and assess chronic effects of environmental quality.*

The monitoring should include productivity, diversity, fecundity, bioaccumulation, and other important aspects of biological species on plots in natural ecosystems (such as a watershed for terrestrial life or a lake or river for aquatic life) and productivity of major agricultural crops, forage, and forests on selected field plots. In addition, periodic regional surveys should be made of those biological species, that indicate trends in environmental quality, including microorganisms in aquatic systems.

Monitoring in watersheds could be designed to reveal effects of land use on water quality and, in so doing, satisfy some of the requirements of

Section 208 of the Clean Water Act. The plans called for in this section would be inadequate without such data on ecological effects. Existing watersheds that are studied by federal and state agencies and universities primarily to understand hydrological processes should also be examined to see if they could be used for monitoring ecological effects (Foebes et al. 1970, NRC 1974).

A long-term commitment is essential to such programs. Evaluations of ecological effects must not be obscured by seasonal or other temporal factors. Without a commitment of 5 to 15 years, such projects are best not begun.

A Word of Caution

The usefulness of all monitoring, be it ambient, source, or effects, depends on the reliability of the measurement process used, the availability of the data once they are obtained, and the analysis of the data. In the next chapter, we discuss the manner in which EPA handles such activities.

REFERENCES

Amdur, M.O. (1977) Toxicological guidelines for research on sulfur oxides and particulates. Pages 48-55, Statistics and the Environment, Proceedings of the Fourth Symposium: A Forum for Interdisciplinary Interaction. March 3-5, 1976, Washington, D.C. Conference sponsored by the American Statistical Association, American Society for Quality Control, and Committee on National Statistics and Committee on Toxicology of the National Academy of Sciences-National Research Council. Washington, D.C.: American Statistical Association.

Beckers, C.V. and S.G. Chamberlain (1974) Design of Cost-Effective Water Quality Surveillance Systems. Socioeconomic Environmental Studies Series, U.S. Environmental Protection Agency, EPA-600/5-746 0004. Washington, D.C.: U.S. Government Printing Office; PB-232 979/5. Springfield, Va.: National Technical Information Service.

Beckers, C.V., S.G. Chamberlain, and G.P. Grimsrud (1972) Quantitative Methods for Preliminary Design of Water Quality Surveillance Systems. By the Raytheon Co. for the U.S. Environmental Protection Agency, EPA-R5-72-001. Washington, D.C.: U.S. Government Printing Office; PB-219 010/6. Springfield, Va.: National Technical Information Service.

Boruch, R.F. and J.S. Cecil (1977) Alternative Methods of Assuring Privacy and Confidentiality in Social Research. Cambridge: Cambridge University Press.

Campbell, D.T., R.F. Boruch, R.D. Schwartz, and J. Steinberg (1975) Confidentiality-preserving modes of access to files and to interfile exchange for useful statistical analysis. Appendix A, Protecting Individual Privacy in Evaluation Research. Committee on Federal Agency Evaluation Research, National Research Council. Washington, D.C.: National Academy of Sciences.

Case, R.A.M., M.E. Hosker, D.B. McDonald, and J.T. Pearson (1954) Tumors of the urinary bladder in workmen engaged in the manufacture and use of certain dyestuff intermediates in the British chemical industry. British Journal of Industrial Medicine 11(2):75-104.

Cobb, E.D. and J.E. Biesecker (1971) The National Hydrologic Bench-mark Network. U.S. Geological Survey Circular 460-D. Washington, D.C.: U.S. Geological Survey.

Cole, P.P. and M.B. Goldman (1975) Occupation. Pages 167-184, Persons at High Risk of Cancer: An Approach to Cancer Etiology and Control, edited by Joseph F. Fraumeni, Jr. New York: Academic Press.

Council on Environmental Quality (1976) Environmental Quality: The Sixth Annual Report of the Council on Environmental Quality. Washington, D.C.: U.S. Government Printing Office.

Crouch, R.L., R.D. Eckert, and D.D. Rugg (1976) Monitoring Groundwater Quality: Economic Framework and Principles. By General Electric Company-TEMPO, Center for Advanced Studies, for the Environmental Monitoring and Support Laboratory, Monitoring Systems Research and Development Division, EPA 600/4-76-045. Las Vegas, Nev.: U.S. Environmental Protection Agency.

Dillaway, R.B. and R. Byerly, Jr. (1976) The Environmental Protection Agency's Research Program, with Primary Emphasis on the Community Health and Surveillance System (CHESS): An Investigative Report. Committee Serial SS, Committee on Science and Technology, U.S. House of Representatives, 94th Congress, 2nd Session. Washington, D.C.: U.S. Government Printing Office.

Discher, D.P., G.D. Kleinman, and F.J. Foster (1975) Pilot Study for Development of an Occupational Disease Surveillance Method. Contract HSM 99-72-69. HEW Publication (NIOSH) #75-162. Office of Health Surveillance and Biometrics. Rockville, Md.: U.S. Department of Health, Education, and Welfare.

Dzubay, T.G. and R.K. Stevens (1973) Applications of x-ray fluorescence to particulate measurements. Pages 211-216, Sensing of Environmental Pollutants. Second Joint Conference, Washington, D.C., December 10-12, 1973. Pittsburgh, Pa.: Instrument Society of America.

Foebes, C., V. Ourybaev, and A.E. Victor (1970) Representative and Experimental Basins, an International Guide for Research and Practice. Studies and Reports in Hydrology No. 4. Paris: UNESCO.

Haenszel, W. (1975) Migrant studies. Pages 361-371, Persons at High Risk of Cancer: An Approach to Cancer Etiology and Control, edited by Joseph F. Fraumeni, Jr. New York: Academic Press.

Harrison, J.W., D.E. Gilbert, P.A. Lawless, and J.H. White (1976) Development Strategy for Pollutant Dosimetry. Chemistry and Physics Laboratory, Air Quality Measurement and Methods Branch, EPA 600/2-76-034. Research Triangle Park, N.C.: U.S. Environmental Protection Agency; PB-256 910/1BE. Springfield, Va.: National Technical Information Service.

Hines, W.G., D.A. Rickert, and S.W. McKenzie (1976) Hydrologic Analysis and River-Quality Data Programs: River-Quality Assessment of the Willamette River Basin, Oregon. Geological Survey Circular 715-D. Reston, Va.: U.S. Geological Survey.

Hines, W.G., D.A. Rickert, S.W. McKenzie, and J.P. Bennett (1975) Formulation and Use of Practical Models for River-Quality Assessment: River-Quality Assessment of the Willamette River Basin, Oregon. Geological Survey Circular 715-B. Reston, Va.: U.S. Geological Survey.

Jennings, M.E., J.O. Shearman, and D.P. Bauer (1976) Selection of Streamflow and Reservior-Release Models for River-Quality Assessment: River-Quality Assessment of the Willamette River Basin, Oregon. Geological Survey Circular 715-E. Reston, Va.: U.S. Geological Survey.

Kinosian, J. (1977) Ambient Air Monitoring Methods. Supplement II, Environmental Monitoring: Analytical Studies for the U.S. Environmental Protection Agency, Volume IV. Report of the Study Group on Environmental Monitoring. National Research Council, Committee on National Statistics, Assembly of Mathematical and Physical Sciences. Washington, D.C.: National Academy of Sciences.

Morgan, M.G. and S.C. Morris (1976) Individual Air Pollution Monitors: An Assessment of National Research Needs. Report of a Workshop on Assessment of Research Needs in Individual Air Pollution Monitors for Ambient Air. July 8-10, 1975, Brookhaven National Laboratory, Upton, N.Y. BNL 50482. Upton, N.Y.: Brookhaven National Laboratory.

Morgan, R.C., P. Guerry, and R.R. Colwell (1976) Antibiotic resistant bacteria in Chesapeake Bay. Chesapeake Science 17(3):216-219.

Moss, M.E. and M.R. Karlinger (1974) Surface water network design by regression analysis simulation. Water Resources Research 10(3):427-433.

National Center for Health Statistics (1968) Use of Vital and Health Records in Epidemiologic Research: A Report of the U.S. National Committee on Vital and Health Statistics. Vital and Health Statistics Series 4, No. 7. Office of Health Statistics. Rockville, Md.: U.S. Department of Health, Education, and Welfare.

National Research Council (1974) International Hydrological Decade Representative and Experimental Basins in the United States: Catalog of Available Data and Results, 1965-72. U.S. National Committee for the International Hydrological Decade. Washington, D.C.: National Academy of Sciences; PB-237 002. Springfield, Va.: National Technical Information Service.

National Research Council (1975) Mineral Resources and the Environment. Committee on Mineral Resources and the Environment. Washington, D.C.: National Academy of Sciences; PB-239 579. Springfield, Va.: National Technical Information Service.

Pitts, J. N., Jr., J.L. Sprung, M. Poe, M.C. Carpelan, and A.C. Lloyd (1976) Corrected South Coast Air Basin oxidant data: some conclusions and implications. Environmental Science and Technology 10(8):794-801.

Rickert, D.A., and W.G. Hines (1975) A Practical Framework for River-Quality Assessment: River Quality Assessment of the Willamette River Basin, Oregon. Geological Survey Circular 715-A. Reston, Va.: U.S. Geological Survey.

Rickert, D.A., W.G. Hines, and S.W. McKenzie (1976a) Methodology for River-Quality Assessment with Application to the Willamette River Basin, Oregon: River-Quality Assessment of the Willamette [River] Basin, Oregon. Geological Survey Circular 715-M. Reston, Va.: U.S. Geological Survey.

Rickert, D.A., W.G. Hines, and S.W. McKenzie (1976b) Project Development and Data Programs for Assessing the Quality of the Willamette River, Oregon: River-Quality Assessment of the Willamette River Basin, Oregon. Geological Survey Circular 715-C. Reston, Va.: U.S. Geological Survey.

Rickert, D.A., V.C. Kennedy, S.W. McKenzie, and W.G. Hines (1976c) A Synoptic Survey of Trace Metals in Bottom Sediments of the Willamette River, Oregon: River-Quality Assessment of the Willamette River Basin, Oregon. Geological Survey Circular 715-F. Reston, Va.: U.S. Geological Survey.

Rickert, D.A., R.R. Petersen, S.W. McKenzie, W.G. Hines, and S.A. Wille (1977) Algal Conditions and the Potential of Future Algal Problems in the Willamette River, Oregon: River-Quality Assessment of the Willamette River Basin, Oregon. Geological Survey Circular 715-G. Reston, Va.: U.S. Geological Survey.

Sanders, T.G., B.B. Berger, and D.D. Adrian (1976) Designing a River Basin Sampling System. Publication No. 62. Amherst, Mass.: Water Resources Research Center, University of Massachusetts.

Shearman, J.O. (1976) Reservoir-System Model for the Willamette River Basin, Oregon: River-Quality Assessment of the Willamette River Basin, Oregon. Geological Survey Circular 715-H. Reston, Va.: U.S. Geological Survey.

Sherwani, J.K. and D.H. Moreau (1975) Strategies for Water Quality Monitoring. UNC-WRRI-75-107 W76-00178. Raleigh, N.C.: North Carolina Water Resources Research Institute; PB-245 765/3GA. Springfield, Va.: National Technical Information Service.

Slap, A.J. (1976) Industrial Users of Philadelphia Treatment Plants. Philadelphia, Pa.: Public Interest Law Center of Philadelphia.

Speizer, F.E., Y. Bishop, and B.G. Ferris (1977) An epidemiologic approach to the study of the health effects of air pollution. Pages 56-68, Proceedings of the Fourth Symposium on Statistics and the Environment, A Forum for Interdisciplinary Interaction. March 3-5, 1976, Washington, D.C. Conference sponsored by the American Statistical Association, American Society for Quality Control, Committee on National Statistics and Committee on Toxicology of the National Academy of Sciences-National Research Council. Washington, D.C.: American Statistical Association.

U.S. Congress, Senate (1972) Senate report 92-724 . . . to accompany H.R. 81-40. Commerce Committee, 92nd Congress, 2nd Session. Pages 2766-2811, United States Code: Congressional and Administrative News. St. Paul: West Publishing Co. (Conference Report 92-175 on pages 2811-2814).

U.S. Environmental Protection Agency (1974) Health Consequences of Sulfur Oxides: A Report from CHESS, 1970-1971. Final Report. National Environmental Research Center, EPA 650/1-74-004. Research Triangle Park, N.C.: U.S. Environmental Protection Agency; PB-234 920/7. Springfield, Va.: National Technical Information Service.

U.S. Environmental Protection Agency (1975a) Model State Water Monitoring Program. Office of Water and Hazardous Materials, Monitoring and Data Support Division. EPA 440/9-74-002. Washington, D.C.: U.S. Environmental Protection Agency.

U.S. Environmental Protection Agency (1975b) Review of the CHESS Program. A Report of a Review Panel of the Science Advisory Board Executive Committee. Washington, D.C.: EPA Science Advisory Board.

U.S. Environmental Protection Agency (1977) Cost Estimates for Construction of Publicly Owned Wastewater Treatment Facilities: 1976 Needs Survey. Office of Water Programs, EPA 430/9-76-010(MCD-48A). Washington, D.C.: U.S. Environmental Protection Agency.

U.S. General Accounting Office (1976a) Better Data Collection and Planning is Needed to Justify Advanced Waste Treatment Construction: Report to the Congress by the Comptroller General. Washington, D.C.: U.S. Government Printing Office.

U.S. General Accounting Office (1976b) Improvements Needed in the Operation and Maintenance of Federally-operated Wastewater Treatment Plants. Washington, D.C.: U.S. Govenment Printing Office.

U.S. Geological Survey (1975) Office of Water Data Coordination. Office of Water Coordination, U.S. Department of the Interior. Reston, Va.: U.S. Geological Survey.

Wallace, L. (1977) Personal Air Quality Monitors. Supplement III, Environmental Monitoring: Analytical Studies for the U.S. Environmental Protection Agency, Volume IV. Report of the Study Group on Environmental Monitoring. National Research Couuncil, Committee on National Statistics, Assembly of Mathematical and Physical Sciences. Washington, D.C.: National Academy of Sciences.

Ward, R.C. (1973) Data Acquisition Systems in Water Quality Management. Socioeconomic Environmental Studies Series, U.S. Environmental Protection Agency, EPA-R5-73-014. Washington, D.C.: U.S. Government Printing Office; PB 222 622/3. Springfield, Va.: National Technical Information Service.

Ward, R.C. and L.R. Freeman (1973) Data requirements of a water quality management program. Water Resources Bulletin 9(6):1234-1248.

3 EPA's Management of Scientific Data

INTRODUCTION

The generation, handling, and uses of scientific data are important functions of EPA. These activities involve three interrelated disciplines: *the measurement process*, which involves sampling and the methods for measuring the environment; *data processing*, wherein computers make data accessible in a desired format; and *analysis and use*, whereby the Agency learns from its data, and applies the derived information to make policy decisions and to improve monitoring programs.

There are many problems associated with EPA's management of scientific data. Some stem from the apparent lack of connection between the data EPA acquires and the decisions the Agency makes. Major problems with EPA's data processing and information handling systems call for a comprehensive review and evaluation. There is often no clear understanding of the beneficiaries or uses of data with the result that data processing systems proliferate and not only monitoring programs suffer. Current quality assurance programs are often inadequate to guarantee that the data produced will be accurate and relevant to decision making. There is much variability in performance among laboratories and a wider program of laboratory certification appears to be needed. Underlying many of these problems is the current scarcity of statistical talent within the Agency.

THE MEASUREMENT PROCESS

We define the environmental measurement process to include all activities associated with the generation of data; i.e., sampling the environment, the choice and application of measurement methods to quantify environmental characteristics, and the application of quality assurance principles to obtain data of required accuracy.

SAMPLING

Before an environmental measurement can be recorded, either a sample of the environment must be isolated and brought to a measuring device, or a measuring instrument must be placed in the environment to obtain an in situ sample. There are many potential variations in the conditions surrounding such operations: varying temperature; air flow or water current patterns; episodic events, such as traffic and storms; possible chemical or biological interferences by other substances; possible alteration of the environment caused by the sampling itself; and changes in the sample during transport.

Decisions must be made concerning the physical size of the sample, location, time of day it is taken, frequency, and type (for example, grab, composite, intermittent, or continuous). The location, timing, and size of the sample required to determine the amount of a pollutant discharged from a specific industrial plant will clearly differ from that required for monitoring pathogenic bacteria in an estuary, or carbon monoxide in the air over an urban area. In selecting a sample, one must also consider the toxicity, abundance, and availability to animals or plants of the pollutants being monitored and distinguish, for example, between those pollutants that may have transient peaks at dangerous levels and those pollutants with a less variable concentration that can be detected at possibly dangerous levels with less frequent sampling. Taking a sample is clearly affected by many factors. To guarantee that the information produced by the sample is objective, careful sampling protocols must be established and maintained.

Definition of Sampling Objectives and Protocols

In the field of environmental monitoring, Congress has provided broad legislative mandates that permit EPA to establish its own choice of monitoring programs and sampling protocols. The Agency therefore has a special responsibility to define its sampling objectives[1] and to maintain standard sampling protocols.

For the sampling objective of surveillance of a particular point source of pollution, EPA provides information on the location, timing, and quantity of the sample to be collected, complete with careful descriptions of the kind of equipment to use.[2] For samples that may be used to provide evidence in legal proceedings, the Agency publishes extensive protocols to protect the integrity of the sample. Much sampling of point sources, however, is not under direct Agency control and depends on the judgment of those taking the sample. And although EPA prescribes in regulations and guidelines criteria for the location of monitoring sites and for the frequency of data collection, individuals responsible for performing the sampling frequently have different incentives from those of EPA and may lack an understanding or appreciation of the importance of their work to the Agency. The CEQ is considering a suggestion for the use of certified "pollution auditors" to assure accuracy of monitoring data reported by industry.

Another sampling objective of the Agency is to determine the temporal and spatial characteristics of pollutant distributions in air or water and to relate these characteristics to sources and to their effects. Here the problems of sampling become complex and very dependent upon recent scientific knowledge. Clearly, before the transport characteristics of pollutants and their physical-chemical interactions can be described, both theory (models) and data must be available. And before the effects of pollutants on man, materials, and biota can be detected, satisfactory models and data are again required. Thus, decisions concerning the type, location, and frequency of sampling become an iterative process, changing as new information and insights become available.

---

[1]Here, we define "sampling objectives" as the immediate goal of the sample, based on which optimal sampling networks can be designed. For example, a sampling network for maintaining surveillance to detect pollution levels in excess of some fixed level can be quite different from one attempting to control pollution over a basin by manipulating sources and different again from one attempting to elucidate cause-and-effect relationships.

[2]The document *Minimal Requirements for a Water Quality Assurance Program* (U.S. EPA 1975c) provides references of relevant EPA publications concerning sampling and analysis; the requirements for recording, storing, and retrieving data; and chain of custody protocols. *Quality Assurance Handbook for Air Pollution Measurement Systems*, Volume II, will provide references relative to air pollution. The *Compliance Monitoring Procedures Handbook*, National Enforcement Investigations Center, EPA Office of Enforcement, details chain of custody procedures.

Design of Sampling Networks

Understanding the environment is the result of a continuing and interactive process. It begins with the knowledge possessed by the analyst to which is added whatever data are available. To describe the environment over a basin or region, one or more models may be postulated and the precision of the desired estimates stated. On this basis, a network of monitoring sites can be chosen and the type and frequency of sampling selected. Discrepancies between the newly observed data and the results predicted by the models usually lead to improved models and, in most cases, to new sampling requirements. This learning process continues until the model and sampling systems meet the objectives of the analyst (Box 1974). Once an adequate model-data sampling network is constructed, it is possible to provide useful forecasts for the region and to institute appropriate environmental pollution controls.

In our survey in Pittsburgh, we found that mathematical models were not commonly used to locate monitoring sites. The primary (and common-sense) considerations appeared to be the location of major water users and dischargers and the current locations of water flow gauges. Sampling periods and methods of analysis differed across various local agencies; and, because the monitoring networks and protocols were not viewed as a single entity, a largely disconnected set of small sampling systems evolved. Greater collaborative efforts are needed to coalesce monitoring programs and sampling protocols over most urban regions.

A sampling system must also be adaptable to emerging or potential problems. Sampling protocols governing the location, timing, and type of sampling and surveillance will change as environmental objectives are achieved and as new objectives are established. Monitoring problems will change with the discovery of new hazards, modified engineering practices, and especially with the development of better models. Models that consider biological factors, sediments, aerosols, trace metals, and organics, as well as chemical and physical properties will generate great demands for good data and appropriate sampling.

With the current state of knowledge, however, it would be premature to publish too many sampling network rules and regulations. The problems of site selection, sampling frequency, and time-dependent mapping are interwoven and are being extensively studied. Much additional work is needed on the application of time series methods. The Agency would do well to finance additional studies in these subject areas. We warn, however, that, unless EPA can provide clear statements of objectives and criteria, such research may be of little value and practical benefits may be delayed.

Central Scientific Responsibility

Responsibility for the study of problems of sampling and for the establishment of sampling networks appears to be diffused throughout the Agency. EPA should establish a central point of scientific responsibility for sampling protocols; network design; processing and audit of sampling activities; and the preparation of guides, instructions, and standards. To do so, EPA must place necessary scientific talent in positions of adequate authority within the Agency. The Office of Science that we propose should assume this responsibility among its others.

The Measurement Method

A measurement method is the analytical procedure used to quantify a particular environmental characteristic. A discussion of the aspects of a measurement method is given in Hunter (1977). In brief, an environmental measurement method should be: (a) readily traceable to national reference standards; (b) specific to the environmental characteristic under study; (c) compatible, where possible, with other measurement methods; (d) capable of eliminating or assessing the effects of interfering phenomena; and (e) not unduly complicated or expensive. A measurement method should also provide statistically valid observations; in other words, the accuracy—both the precision and bias—of the observations should be determined.

EPA requires a large quantity and diversity of environmental measurements. In addition to the six criteria air pollutants (sulfur dioxide, nitrogen dioxide, ozone, carbon monoxide, total suspended particulates, and hydrocarbons) and characteristics commonly used to measure water quality (for example, biochemical oxygen demand, pH, dissolved oxygen, total dissolved solids, phosphates, coliform bacteria, and suspended solids), there are numerous organic and inorganic chemicals, biological substances, and radioactive compounds that require surveillance. The list of pollutants and potential pollutants grows steadily.

The standardization of measurement methods is essential to all scientific work. EPA has therefore established a *reference* measurement method for each pollutant required by regulation to be monitored. A reference measurement method is an authorized single protocol which describes how a sample of the pollutant should be taken and includes a description of the instruments and procedures to be used in making a measurement.

The development of a reference measurement method usually requires years of collaborative work. Unfortunately, to meet the deadlines established by the Clean Air Amendments of 1970, the Agency was compelled to produce reference methods for the criteria air pollutants in great haste. For some of the air pollution characteristics, no satisfactory measurement methods were available at the time the amendments were enacted; and, for other characteristics, several alternative methods were available. Not surprisingly, much controversy attended the initial publication of the air pollutant reference methods. For example, the proposed measurement method for nitrogen dioxide had to be withdrawn.[3] Similar problems have attended reference methods for measuring pollutants in water.

The establishment of a reference measurement method involves many sciences. Physics and chemistry play an essential role in structuring the measurement system and in choosing its metric. The choice of instruments and the techniques for taking and handling samples require field and laboratory experience. Other aspects of the measurement method, as specified in the beginning of this section, also require collaborative work by scientists and engineers in many disciplines. Given the many problems and extreme time pressures, reference measurement methods have been developed by acknowledged professionals within EPA in as reasonable a manner as could be expected.

Concomitant with the establishment of reference measurement methods is the manufacture of Standard Reference Materials (SRM), materials with accuracies often orders of magnitude higher than the common laboratory standards used in day-to-day calibration of reference measurement methods. The SRMs are essential to nationwide standardization of the performance of a measurement method and provide each laboratory with the means to trace its own measurements to the ultimate standards maintained by the National Bureau of Standards (NBS). The NBS has developed over 40 SRMs for the special needs of the environmental scientist. Unfortunately, there are no SRMs for many environmental pollutants, particularly the pesticides. EPA and NBS have discussed the need for and cost of development and manufacture of SRMs and how to implement traceability. As part of its own quality assurance program, EPA also has a program for the manufacture and distribution of its own reference standards.

In addition to certified data that are provided with SRMs, evaluated data on physical and chemical properties of pure compounds can also serve as reference data in the development of monitoring methodology.

---

[3]A description of the reference methods for the six criteria air pollutants is given in a paper, "Ambient Air Monitoring Methods," prepared by John Kinosian (1977) for the Study Group on Environmental Monitoring. See Appendix E for an abstract and for the availability of this paper.

Sectroscopic data are one example. EPA has built up capability of accessing such data, which are part of the government-wide National Standard Reference Data System. This system, which is coordinated by the Office of Standard Reference Data at NBS, is a resource for many evaluated data on compounds and systems relevant to environmental pollution. It is useful for development of monitoring methods and even more so for research in the development of models, for example, in better determinations of rates of reaction.

Statistical Attributes

The numerical data produced by a measurement method should meet statistical criteria. The data produced within a laboratory should give estimates of the actual level of the pollutant with either zero or small bias (the average deviation of measurements from the "true" value). Furthermore, the data produced by each laboratory should have good precision; in other words, the variance (or some other statistical measure of the variability of repeated observations) should be small. The measurements should be stable, not subject to frequent aberrant observations. Also, it is helpful if the distribution of repeated observations is known.

For many reference measurement methods, no estimates of precision or bias exist. For those methods for which estimates of precision and bias are published, many are based on data that are years old. Examples for water can be found in the *Federal Register* (U.S. EPA 1973c), entitled EPA's "Guidelines Establishing Test Procedures for Analysis of Pollutants." Of the approximately 90 measurement methods provided, only a third had precision and bias statements constructed from complete interlaboratory studies; and 16 had neither precision nor bias statements. There are now literally dozens of measurement methods specified by the Agency as reference methods for which no measures of bias or precision are available. In addition, the list of pollutants and their associated approved measurement methods continues to grow. Of course, it is recognized that the urgency to publish approved methods, as required by law, has often prohibited thorough studies. It is widely accepted, however, that the merit of the data depends heavily on measures of precision and bias of the measurement methods used. The Agency clearly needs to expand studies of the precision and bias of its many reference measurement methods.

For many environmental characteristics, the Agency selected measurement methods already developed by the American Society for Testing and Materials (ASTM), the U.S. Geological Survey, and other organizations. EPA often made small changes in these protocols before listing them as reference methods or equivalent methods. Unfortunately, even small changes can have a profound influence on the precision of measurements, and collaborative work to study the consequences of these modifications remains to be done.

In fact, all reference methods should be submitted to *ruggedness testing*,[4] formal investigations of the consequences that small changes in analysis protocols have on the measurements that are obtained.

In addition, components of error analyses of mathematical functions that appear in most reference method protocols should be explored. For example, the measured concentration of a pollutant is often expressed as a mathematical function of observations on volume, temperature, flow rates, and other factors, each of which introduces its own variability of measurement. Both ruggedness testing and components of error analyses can contribute substantially to identifying the sources of variability in observations produced by a measurement method. This identification may lead to ways to reduce variability.

Compatibility of Alternative Methods

Reference methods authorized by EPA acquire a stature and permanence beyond those of other methods, although many alternative measurement methods appear to do very well in meeting the needs of state and local agencies.[5] The Agency often does indicate that some alternative measurement methods are equivalent to its chosen method in that they give results that agree sufficiently closely. Very few studies of the compatibility, or equivalence, of these alternative methods are available, however. The unfortunate competitiveness that sometimes exists between proponents of alternative measurement methods should be replaced by collaborative studies to determine their degree of compatibility. The evolution of acceptable measurement methods requires the continuing

[4]Ruggedness testing, a term first used by W.J. Youden of the National Bureau of Standards, is described in more detail in Hunter (1977).

[5]EPA recommends that gas bubblers, the reference method for monitoring sulfur dioxide, constitute at least half of a regional network to monitor the pollutant and that they be used along with continuous monitors. Allegheny County's monitoring network for sulfur dioxide has seven telemetered continuous monitors and no gas bubblers. The County has an extensive Huey Plate (sulfation rate) network to monitor ambient sulfur dioxide. The sulfation rate method was the first widely used method to monitor sulfur dioxide and was in use by the County as early as 1930. Allegheny County continued using this method because of its very low cost and the value of the data to indicate changes over a long term and to identify "hot spots." The County has obtained good correlation between sulfation rates and concentrations of sulfur dioxide, but Huey Plate (sulfation rate) monitoring is not an approved method.

study of alternatives and less emphasis on identification of a "one and only" method.

Interlaboratory Variability

There is often less variation between repeated measurements taken within a laboratory than what occurs in those taken at different laboratories. To measure and control these sources of variability, organizations such as the ASTM regularly conduct interlaboratory testing programs. EPA has also instituted interlaboratory comparison programs for some pollution characteristics. Recent studies conducted within the Agency have demonstrated widespread variability between separate EPA laboratories using the same reference measurement methods on standard samples. The results of these studies are not generally accessible to the public, and thus the users of pollution measurements in other agencies and industry are unable to determine readily the actual magnitude of the variability of pollution measurements made at EPA. An understanding of the usefulness of a measurement method is not complete without interlaboratory investigations to discover and measure the variability emanating from all organizations associated with the practice of the method. At the same time, care should be exercised to ensure that the acknowledgment of variability, particularly between laboratories, is not used to disparage the Agency's efforts to establish measurement methods.

Before EPA was established, the field performance of many water measurement methods was determined by large interlaboratory studies, often involving more than 100 governmental, industrial, and private laboratories, in programs run by the Analytical Reference Service of the Division of Water Pollution Control of the U.S. Public Health Service. Each participating laboratory was sent one or more "standard samples" for analysis. The results were then assembled and studied. Both the variability of measurements across laboratories and the variability within each laboratory were published and distributed to all the participants. Measurements were appropriately coded to protect confidentiality. It was thus possible for each laboratory to check its own performance against the performance of others.

EPA conducts similar interlaboratory performance surveys to estimate and reduce the variability existing between laboratories. Semi-annual performance surveys involving approximately 100 laboratories have been conducted for several air characteristics (SO_2, NO_2, CO, SO_4, NO_3); and similar studies have been performed for water characteristics, pesticides, and radionuclides (Bromberg et al. 1975, U.S. EPA 1976a, Ballinger et al. 1972, U.S. EPA 1975e, U.S. EPA 1975b).[6]

It is generally accepted that such interlaboratory surveys have beneficial effects. Early surveys (1972–73) of measurement methods for air characteristics uncovered wide variation in laboratory performance. On one occasion, only 60 percent of the participants provided test results within acceptable limits. More recent surveys have demonstrated a marked reduction in the number of "outlier" laboratory performances.

It is important to remember that these reported surveys only describe the analytical variability associated with a measurement method for a particular pollutant characteristic, and usually do not include measures of variability due to sampling and sample handling. Furthermore, most of these interlaboratory performance surveys are voluntary and, inadequate resources are allocated for follow-up studies to assist laboratories that performed poorly, although EPA does recognize the value of such studies. Finally, only a subset of the known important pollution characteristics are currently studied as part of regular interlaboratory performance surveys.

There is clearly a need for interlaboratory comparison programs involving major environmental characteristics and covering many more laboratories. One indication of the necessity for these programs is that tens of thousands of National Pollution Discharge Elimination System (NPDES) permits issued by EPA, under the Federal Water Pollution Control Act Amendments of 1972 (PL 92-500), require those organizations discharging pollutants into the nation's waters to self-monitor and to report on their performance. Measurement methods for a great variety of pollutant characteristics are thus being inaugurated in numerous laboratories across the nation. Accurately assessing the progress of this management of environmental pollution requires that the Agency standardize and control these varied measurement methods. This work has only begun. As a partial solution to the problem, we recommend later in this chapter a certification program for those laboratories that ascertain compliance with permits or standards.

Quality Assurance

The main objective of the precision and bias studies and the interlaboratory surveys described above is the estimation and ultimate control of the variability associated with the measurement *method* itself.

[6]See also Logsdon, J.O. and M.J. Carter (1976) Comparison of Ambient Air Quality Monitoring Data from Co-located Sampling Sites. Central Regional Laboratory. Chicago, Ill.: U.S. Environmental Protection Agency. (Unpublished)

Largely ignored by such investigations as are done are the additional contributions to variability of the measurement *process* caused by sampling, sample handling, the use of different instruments and reagents, the differing abilities of analysts, and the quality of laboratory support facilities. These factors have not been ignored by EPA, but their development and implementation has been severely limited by the lack of resources. Further, only persistent attention can insure the quality of samples over extended periods. Effective surveillance of sampling protocols requires simultaneous (split) sampling programs and other independent checks to guarantee that the sample reflects the environment from which it was taken. The problems of estimation, surveillance, and control of all the sources of variability—that is, the control of the measurement process—is a function of the newly established quality assurance programs within EPA.

An example of the importance of quality assurance programs can be seen in the results of a recent survey of the St. Louis Regional Air Monitoring System (RAMS) of the St. Louis Regional Air Pollution Study (U.S. EPA 1976a), a special investigation designed to aid in the development of mathematical models useful for forecasting air pollution concentrations as a function of source emissions, solar radiation, and the weather. The study is unique and was specifically planned to elucidate the problems of model development appropriate to an urban or rural region (Burton and Hidy 1974). The study requires extensive time traces of high quality monitoring data. To ensure the validity of such data, careful sampling and calibration protocols were established for the monitoring sites. In a quality assurance audit of the St. Louis RAMS, independent sample measurements of pollutants were obtained using additional equipment, and audits of in situ instruments were obtained using portable calibration equipment. Even though sampling and analysis protocols had been carefully set down for this research project, measurement process variability in excess of acceptable limits was common and corrective actions were required (Jurgens and Rhodes 1975).

This example is instructive because it indicates that, even when careful sampling protocols are decreed, reference measurement methods are available, and a project is run with excellent data as one of its principal objectives, the conduct of both sampling and measurement requires careful and persistent surveillance if dependable data are to result.

Surveillance, such as that conducted in St. Louis, forms only a part of a measurement process quality assurance program. If a reliable sampling and measurement method program is to be maintained, there is an obvious need for the issuance and documentation of sampling and reference method procedures that are clear in their exposition and consistent in their approach. To determine precision and bias of measurement methods, sufficient quantities of reference sample materials must be supplied to support interlaboratory programs. Standard laboratory materials and equipment must be studied and recommended. There is need for standard protocols for the identification, handling, computation, and storage of laboratory data. There is also need to train personnel in laboratory quality control procedures.

The Agency's current fledgling quality assurance program is an effort to meet these diverse needs. EPA recommends that 10 to 20 percent of the cost of a monitoring program be committed to quality assurance activities. We have already noted that the Agency conducts interlaboratory studies of several reference measurement methods and that such studies are a part of the development of new reference methods. In addition, the Agency has initiated a program to establish uniform language and definition of terms, as evidenced by the publication of a recently distributed handbook for air characteristics (von Lehmden and Nelson 1976) and an earlier EPA document for water (Ballinger et al. 1972). (The latter document relates to quality control within the laboratory and should be brought up to date and broadened to embrace interlaboratory quality problems and quality assurance in general.) There is, however, no central office in the Agency with suffcient scientific resources to insure uniformity of definitions and protocols. Nor is there any real authority and independence for those who do have quality assurance responsibilities; they may "advise" or "view with alarm," but otherwise they have little control.

The quality assurance activities within the Agency are understaffed and effectively uncoordinated. The failure to ensure scientific control over the measurement process is bound to injure the Agency in its forensic activities and in managing the environment and demonstrating improvements in environmental quality. Perhaps most important of all, the reputation of the Agency as a scientific organization concerned with valid measurements of environmental characteristics will suffer in the absence of an aggressive quality assurance program. The current quality assurance activities of the Agency, while a step in the right direction, need much additional attention and support.

LABORATORY CERTIFICATION

The Safe Drinking Water Act of 1974 calls for the establishment of regulations that specify maximum permissible levels for contaminants in the nation's primary drinking water. The Act also calls for the setting of criteria and for procedures that will insure compliance with regulations.

Section 140(1) of the Act defines a "primary drinking water regulation" as one that includes "quality control and testing procedures."

Drawing on the reference to quality control and testing procedures and recognizing the important role that laboratory analyses must play in any system of compliance, operation, and maintenance, EPA (U.S. EPA 1975f) provided a regulation stating: "Samples may be considered only if they have been analyzed by a laboratory approved by the state . . . ." In the preamble to Part 141 of this regulation, the Agency further states: "EPA will develop as soon as possible, in cooperation with the States and other interested parties, criteria and procedures for laboratory certification." We note that the literal use of the words "laboratory certification" does not derive from a specific instruction on the part of Congress but is inferred from the powers provided by the Safe Drinking Water Act.

The Agency has already embarked on a national program of laboratory certification. Its entrance into this area is not a first for a federal agency. The Clinical Laboratory Improvement Act authorized the certification of laboratories by the Center for Disease Control, and the Social Security Administration (20 CFR 405) may also specify criteria for the certification of Medicare laboratories. The National Bureau of Standards has a Measurement Assurance Program to assist laboratories in training staff, in providing measurement protocols, and in establishing uniform data analysis systems.

A process of certification is planned for the ten regional laboratories of EPA. An initial review of the quality assurance status of these laboratories began early in 1976 under a directive from Assistant Administrator John Quarles (December 24, 1975), following an agency review of monitoring activities in 1975. A draft plan proposes that, once regional laboratories have been approved, the Administrator will delegate to the regional administrators the authority to certify primary state laboratories under rules he will provide to assure national uniformity. These rules form the National Quality Assurance Program for Laboratory Certification (NQAPLC). The states, in turn, will certify local laboratories. Commercial laboratories will be certified in much the same way as those used by the states are certified.

The draft program for laboratory certification of water supply laboratories envisions the formation of evaluation teams composed of a microbiologist, an analytical chemist, a radiochemist (there is some doubt whether all regions can supply one), and a sanitary engineer. Responsibility for evaluating the quality assurance aspects of the certification program through the use of check samples, the evaluation of record maintenance, and the application of laboratory quality control procedures will rest with the Regional Quality Assurance Coordinator.

The draft Procedures and Criteria Technical Manuals are listings of minimum requirements to be checked. Topics include: personnel experience and academic background, laboratory equipment and instrument specifications, sample handling protocols, and quality control procedures, along with general laboratory procedures and facilities. For the measurement of drinking water characteristics, only those analytical techniques designated by EPA are to be used.

The requirements for certification are mainly designed to insure that the available laboratory equipment, personnel, and procedures are adequate. For the purpose of intralaboratory data quality assurance, at least one duplicate sample is to be run every ten samples. How the results of these duplicate analyses are to be reviewed is currently left to the judgment of the local quality control personnel.

For all water quality characteristics measured at least once a year, the certification protocol requires the laboratory to process and report on an unknown performance standard at least once a year and a known reference standard either quarterly or, for some chemical characteristics, at least once a year. These results are to be judged by control limits set up by EPA, which is to supply the performance and reference standard materials.

Once the hardware and personnel credentials of a laboratory have passed initial certification review, the major emphasis of subsequent certification audits will be on day-to-day laboratory performance. If there is an active quality assurance program within each laboratory and those responsible for quality assurance review have proper statistical training and experience, then the number of times that sample analyses are reproduced *within* each laboratory appears ample for the control of intralaboratory measurement processes. There is some question, however, whether sufficient information concerning good performance *across* certified laboratories can be secured using check samples distributed only once a quarter or less frequently.

The certification of laboratories is viewed as an important step forward by the Agency. It is desirable that the certification program be expanded to include additional environmental characteristics beyond those linked to drinking water.

  • *We recommend that a continuing certification program be established for those laboratories that, by performing measurements, determine whether industries and state and local governments are complying with permits or standards related to all EPA programs. Such certification should be based on performance, not merely on evaluations of personnel, equipment, and methods.*

DATA PROCESSING AND INFORMATION HANDLING SYSTEMS

EPA has a broad range of responsibilities. They include sponsoring environmental research, setting standards, writing permits, enforcing regulations, detecting violators, determining changes in environmental quality, and monitoring. Most of these activities have an associated data system (a data processing or information handling system), often several. Occasionally, systems attempt to serve more than one need. Our purpose is to review and comment on the current state of EPA's data processing and information handling operations.

Most of EPA's data systems have evolved through several stages. When the Agency was formed, it assumed responsibility for several existing data systems. As a matter of expediency, EPA did not establish a comprehensive plan for its data processing and information handling operations but, instead, made a number of interagency agreements and contracts with commercial companies to meet pressing needs. Since then, much of the Agency's internal energy has been spent organizing the various data systems within each of its separate zones of responsibility and, generally, "running to catch up" with local needs. The result has been a heterogeneous proliferation of data systems in EPA that guarantees less than optimal benefits. EPA imposes this fragmentation on state and local agencies that must meet EPA requirements for reporting data. This fragmentation prevents state and local agencies from achieving internal harmony among data systems and blocks the coordination of data systems on a national scale.

Although a diversity of computer equipment, vendor services, and data processing and information handling operations can have practical as well as technical justification in some cases, the unnecessary proliferation within EPA and between EPA and other agencies implies increased cost of management and use, as well as increased cost to train staff and users of the systems. Some of this proliferation is a direct result of the current procedure of submitting an RFP (Request for Proposal) and selecting the lowest bidder rather than the one who best meets a well defined set of needs. To substitute criteria other than the lowest cost implies that the Agency has the staff to prepare criteria related to EPA needs and to evaluate bids against these criteria. EPA may not have sufficient, qualified staff to follow this approach.

TABLE 3.1 Major EPA Data Processing and Information Handling Systems and Costs

Type of System	Number of Systems	Annual Costs in Thousands of Dollars			
		Computer	Personnel	Contractors	Total
Data acquisition	19	$3,735	$2,455	$2,294	$8,484
Administration	13	2,508	993	301	3,802
Information handling	7	916	89	1,350	2,355
Modeling	5	894	405	810	2,109
	44	$8,053	$3,942	$4,755	$16,750

SOURCE: Libster (1976).

TYPES OF EPA DATA SYSTEMS AND THEIR COST

Table 3.1 lists both those current EPA data systems and those under development for which computer costs "generally" exceeded $20,000 in FY 1975 (Libster 1976). Excluded is an estimated annual cost of more than $1 million for network services and payments to contractors to prepare planning or evaluation studies.

The most expensive EPA data processing system is Storage and Retrieval for Water Quality Data (STORET). In FY 1975, costs for computer hardware, staff, and abstractors totaled $2,196,000. The system already stores 40 million observations and is growing at a rate of 8 million observations per year. Forty-three states make use of the system. Of the 200,000 stations with records in the file, 83,000 are active.

Second to STORET, in terms of FY 1975 cost for hardware, staff, and contractors, is the Pesticides Analysis Retrieval Control System (PARCS), which cost $892,000. Next is the Population Studies System, which cost $831,000. The important system, the Storage and Retrieval of Aerometric Data (SAROAD), cost $819,000. The most expensive modeling capability was the Strategic Environmental Assessment System (SEAS), which cost $1,429,000. As of July 1976, SEAS had been denied continued funding for FY 1977 by the Office of Management and Budget. The most expensive administrative system is the Integrated Financial Management System (FMS), which cost $899,000. It is followed by the Personnel/Payroll System (DIPS) at $777,000. The most expensive information handling system is the Pesticides Registration System, which cost $636,000.

In examining the priorities implied in the allocation of resources among the four categories shown in Table 3.1, we are compelled to ask if there are sufficient resources allocated to staff in the important areas of data acquisition, information handling, data analysis and reports, and modeling. An equally important long-term consideration is the allocation of resources for equipment, staff, and use of contractors. It appears that EPA may lack sufficient qualified staff, since the Agency appears dependent upon outside contractors to develop and operate their data systems.

In considering the number of data systems and the cost of their operation, one must also consider the much larger cost (maybe tenfold) for data collection. Costs of data collection are even much greater than costs of computer hardware or software. We estimate that a station monitoring the six criteria air pollutants requires a man-year of work annually to operate the station, to evaluate and calibrate instruments, to prepare reagents, and to transcribe data from strip charts. The annual cost of this data collection, including salaries, is about $40,000. At such a station, we estimate that total suspended particulates are measured every six days and that each of the other five criteria air pollutants is measured continuously. Hourly average concentrations of each of these five pollutants are reported each hour, except for an average of a few hours each day when the instruments are being adjusted or calibrated or are inoperative because of malfunctions. Thus about 40,000 measurements are obtained each year from such a station, and the cost is about $1 per observation. If manual rather than automatic measurement instruments are used, the cost is substantially higher.

Clearly the data are expensive. Are these costs balanced by a corresponding benefit to society? When one contemplates the many environmental characteristics now being monitored and the cost of gathering these data, the need for even the simplest kind of studies to improve cost–effectiveness becomes evident.

REVIEW AND EVALUATION OF EPA DATA SYSTEMS

To evaluate the effectiveness of existing EPA data systems, it will be necessary to undertake a basic and comprehensive study of operations in the larger context of monitoring programs. It is also essential that top management be involved in the creation of effective monitoring programs by assuming responsibility for establishing objectives and criteria to guide their development. In this section, we will discuss some of the problems with EPA's data processing and information handling operations, recommend possible solutions, and draw up a comprehensive evaluative approach.

The current data systems within EPA can be characterized as follows:

- Many varied data systems exist that are separate and uncoordinated.
- Impressive descriptions are given of hardware and software.
- There is no clear identification of the purposes or the beneficiaries of specific data or information from a given monitoring program.
- There is no provision for assigning priorities to unmet needs, particularly to measures for improving data from current monitoring programs.
- Little evaluation is done of how well the data systems currently contribute to managing the environment, detecting violators, analyzing trends, or solving scientific and policy problems.
- The primary function and uses of many EPA computer-based data systems are unclear, regardless of whether the principal users are states, regional EPA offices, EPA management, or others.
- There is an imbalance favoring data systems for physical and chemical environmental characteristics, while many biological data are not available through computer systems.
- Primary emphasis has been on establishing and maintaining data handling (storage and retrieval) capabilities without adequate emphasis given to the quality of the data or to the uses of the data for analysis and other purposes of environmental management.
- Little consideration is apparently being given to the use of statistical designs to improve the collection of data, the quality of data, or the efficiency of maintaining, storing, and retrieving data.

Specific examples of these types of problems are not difficult to find. Problems with STORET point to the need for planning, coordination, and clearly defined objectives at all levels of initiating and operating a data system. STORET experienced delays in implementing hardware and software after awarding its current vendor the contract for computer services. Part of the explanation for such a delay is that a new company that is unfamiliar with the kinds of problems posed by this system may not think to charge for solving them unless they have been clearly specified by EPA. An experienced vendor includes charges for these problems in their bid, and is therefore at a disadvantage. STORET is now going to change its vendor again.

STORET has also stored data in inefficient manners. In FY 1975, $1.1 million was paid to a vendor for the direct cost of computer services. Over one-fourth of this amount went to the rental fees for disc storage because data were stored on-line, a costly and often unnecessary way to store data. Storing data, especially those not frequently used, on tapes or by other means would be less expensive. In addition, there are ways to store data in a hierarchial structure so that they could be retrieved more efficiently for their most commonly used purposes.

STORET accepts any data that users enter. For lack of a better place to store effluent data, states have been entering data on effluents along with those on ambient water quality. Not all this effluent data is clearly marked, making for difficult and possibly inaccurate analyses. In addition, the proliferation of data in STORET makes it difficult to conduct special studies. To study changes in water quality during the past decade in 200 municipal areas, CEQ had to screen the data from 61,000 stations located in or near these municipal areas to determine whether the data met criteria suitable for the study. Only data from 200 stations in about 30 cities were found to meet these criteria. Searching through such a large data set to separate useful from irrelevant data is an expensive procedure, especially if the data have not been previously audited.

For SAROAD, EPA's ambient air quality data bank, the vendor of computer hardware was changed from one company to another. The change began in 1974 and took over a year to complete. Because it was apparently poorly planned, few data could be obtained during the period of transition, except by means of costly special programming efforts. Data were effectively lost for a complete year, because the software that had previously been used for data management was incompatible with the new hardware.

Lack of clear operational objectives or clearly defined beneficiaries leads to other problems, as illustrated by the experience with EPA's General Point Source File (GPSF). It was designed as a flexible, multi-purpose system, primarily intended to keep track of NPDES permits and schedules of compliance with construction of pollution abatement equipment and to store data on water quality characteristics of effluents that dischargers are required to monitor. Attempts were made to incorporate an unrealistic amount of data into the system, with the result that costs ballooned. In addition, it had problems with its complex software, and the system lost data. Ironically, EPA's enforcement division, which had originally motivated development of GPSF, later indicated that it had needed the system for one simple purpose: to keep track of the types of letters indicating compliance with pollution abatement schedules and the dates by which it was to receive them. The division developed its own computer system to handle these matters.

Until emphasis is given to the collection of data that are relevant to specific purposes, criticism of EPA monitoring programs will continue to be justified. We are not impressed with software or hardware evaluations that ignore how the data are finally put to use for environmental management, as in determining trends or resolving scientific or policy problems. Furthermore, in a dynamic field such as the environment, data needs will change as problems change or as new insights are gained. Yet we have not found provisions for data evaluations or documentation that indicate how to adapt data storage requirements to these changing needs.

Surprisingly, it has been difficult to obtain information that would lead to an understanding of the actual role or contribution of specific data systems. There is ample documentation of immediate objectives of individual systems; but concise statements, based on actual uses of the data, that identify the agencies or individuals who benefit from the data and the ways in which they benefit are largely unavailable.

We were disappointed to see that so few resources were committed to auditing data to assess or ensure the quality and timeliness of data being stored and retrieved. Such auditing should be an integral part of the design and operation of a monitoring program. Stratified sampling designs should be employed. It is our firm belief that, unless data being collected in the field meet an identifiable need of the group collecting the data—whether a federal, interstate, state, or local agency—and unless those collecting the data clearly understand the ultimate uses that will be made of them, their quality, timeliness, and usefulness must be suspect.

Definition of Priorities and Objectives

Each year since the formation of EPA, at least one major EPA data system has been introduced, changed, or converted. Receptivity to change is natural to the Agency. The approach to change, however, has been fragmented; each data system has been developed or modified to satisfy the needs of a particular EPA division or monitoring program, without considering the associated needs of other divisions or of the Agency as a whole.

Improving data systems will not be easy in an organization that has been emphasizing the use of contractors to promote elaborate hardware and software configurations without a clear definition of objectives. Sufficient time and effort have not been allocated to develop a list of Agency priorities based on sound scientific management. Instead, there is a surprising amount of energy devoted to generating justifications without context. The rationale behind creating data processing systems commonly has been the need to publish reports required by diverse laws, to supply reports requested by EPA itself, and to provide quantitative information of supposed scientific and historic value. Although a simple justification stating that the data are needed to implement legislation may have been excusable when EPA was first formed, such a justification should no longer be accepted as a basis for large and expensive monitoring programs and data systems.

Failure to review data systems in the larger context of the monitoring programs of which they are a part will perpetuate the current unsatisfactory approach and ultimately result in greater cost and questionable effectiveness.

Before considering specific recommendations, we recognized that EPA is part of the political process. The Agency is often asked to respond quickly and to supply valid data to meet unanticipated or changing conditions. Further, it is expensive to modify existing procedures and data systems. The recommendations made here are intended to help EPA invest resources in computer-aided monitoring and in data processing and information handling operations that are responsive to the Agency's changing needs. Our recommendation in Chapter 2, that EPA develop prototype designs for new or modified monitoring networks, applies to data collection procedures and data processing operations as well.

• *We recommend that prior to establishing or changing either a data collection procedure of a national monitoring program or a data processing or information handling operation, EPA develop and evaluate prototypes to ensure that data, collection procedures, and computer systems effectively meet specified needs.*

Priority should be given to the development of a system only if the uses to be made of the data for environmental management are clearly indicated and if the design of the system enables periodic evaluation of the data and data processing systems. The development of prototypes should be done cooperatively with state and local agencies and professional scientific organizations.

Another of our major recommendations is the result of our investigation of serious problems and inadequacies concerning monitoring and data systems. There have been many studies of existing and proposed data systems, including interviews of so-called users (such as the data collectors and processors) of data systems. Little attention has been paid, however, to answering the basic question about who the current and intended beneficiaries are, that is, those who use the data for environmental management. A proper evaluation of data systems requires that this and other basic questions about monitoring programs be answered.

• *We recommend that an in-depth review and evaluation be made for each current and proposed data processing or information handling system of the*

Agency in conjunction with its associated monitoring programs. This review requires that EPA answer these basic questions:

•• *Who are the current and potential beneficiaries of the data and the computer systems?*

•• *What are the specific short-term and long-term benefits?*

•• *How do the data and the data systems contribute to environmental management?*

•• *What high priority needs of the Agency do they meet?*

Review and Evaluation

Once EPA management has clearly identified priorities for the end uses of data collection, data processing operations, computer systems, and data analysis, we recommend that each data processing system be reviewed and evaluated along the following lines:

• uses of both the data and the data processing system in (a) developing and evaluating pollution control strategies, (b) developing and validating models to understand environmental problems and to predict the impact of new pollution sources, and (c) establishing and achieving standards for the quality of the data;

• necessary frequency of data collection;

• guidelines for the participation of users in the design and evaluation of data processing systems;

• usefulness of EPA data processing systems for research purposes;

• relationship of EPA data processing systems to state and federal users;

• overlap or duplication with other EPA data processing or information handling systems and with those of state, local, and other federal agencies;

• compatibility of EPA data processing systems with those of other federal agencies, with respect to codes used to identify data;

• adequacy of data identification to determine (a) source and other ancillary data; (b) types of instruments employed and the quality, precision, and bias of the measurements; and (c) prevailing conditions influencing the quality of data collection;

• length of time that data is kept in current computer files compared to less costly storage for possible later use in historical analysis;

• extent of decentralization of data editing or storage that is desirable; and

 • software availability and development.

We also advise that the four basic questions in our recommendation be answered before any additional studies of EPA data systems are undertaken by EPA or by contractors that review or plan computer systems for the Agency.

Who Should Conduct Review?

This review and evaluation should be conducted by the EPA Office of Science that we propose be established (see Chapter 4). The analysis must be made by a full-time professional group; it cannot be adequately done by part-time advisory groups such as the EPA Science Advisory Board or committees of the National Research Council. The group should include experts in: (a) management, design, and operation of large data processing systems; (b) data collection and analysis; and (c) environmental problems. Except for the staff of the proposed EPA Office of Science, the review group should include only as many of the staff of EPA as are necessary to provide information. Furthermore, this group should not consist of employees of only one consulting firm, equipment manufacturer, or university. We believe it is not in EPA's best interests to depend on the staff of a single contractor or organization to perform the proposed study, because objectivity and freedom to evaluate or recommend may be jeopardized if future contract opportunities are at stake. The study should also involve the Administrator and senior management of EPA, so that overall priorities and needs can be identified.

The evaluation group should report directly to the Administrator of EPA. It should be independent of the EPA Management Information and Systems Division to maintain objectivity and to avoid the narrow focus characteristic of reports and evaluations associated with that Division.

We urge that provisions be made for a continuing evaluation of the effectiveness of data systems by groups of independent experts including those in environmental agencies at all levels of government. These activities should also be coordinated by the Office of Science.

DATA ANALYSIS AND DISSEMINATION

ANALYSIS OF ENVIRONMENTAL DATA

If it is to make informed decisions, EPA must analyze the data it requires to be collected or assure that others are analyzing them. In particular, the

Agency should attempt to relate its data to data on health and ecological effects gathered by other agencies. This type of study should indicate ways in which data collection efforts could be improved and may assist in the discovery of relationships between substances released to the environment and their subsequent effects.

It appears, however, that most data acquired by EPA through environmental monitoring programs are not analyzed adequately. This suspicion is fostered by inordinate delays in publishing data, programs in which myriad data are not available through a computer system, reports that list summary values from stations with no interpretation of the data (as in some annual reports on air quality trends), unnecessary monitoring, and designs for monitoring systems that are not based on data.

Furthermore, comparative analyses of environmental data and data on effects from different agencies depend on the interest and initiative of the staff of the agencies and receive no official recognition or special allocation of funds. Therefore, these activities are sporadic. EPA maintains many large environmental data banks, including those for ambient water quality (STORET), ambient air quality (SAROAD), sources of air pollutants (NEDS), and pesticides (PARCS). Systems will also be established for storing information on the nation's drinking water supplies and on sources of water pollutants. Little effort has been made to relate these data to data on health and ecological effects, although opportunities exist to do so, for example, with the following: data on morbidity and mortality from the National Center for Health Statistics (NCHS); data on cancer from the National Cancer Institute (NCI); data on veterans receiving a pension or compensation for illnesses from the Veterans Administration; and data on federally assisted medical treatment within Professional Standard Review Organization units from the Department of Health, Education, and Welfare.

Some data must be analyzed in making sound decisions. The decision to ban aldrin and dieldrin was based on analysis of data from three different monitoring programs indicating the widespread presence of these pesticides in air, food, and human tissue. Some data, upon examination, may provide assurance that there are no pollution problems, and there may appear to be no need to analyze them further. Since data collection is expensive, however, EPA should determine that data not only have clearly intended purposes and meet them efficiently but also serve as many purposes as possible.

An important way in which EPA could do so is to analyze its environmental data in relation to various purposes they could serve, such as measuring the progress of environmental programs in terms of improvements in environmental quality, studying relationships between pollution and its effects, and evaluating national monitoring networks.

• *We recommend that EPA analyze its environmental data for the purposes of evaluating environmental management policies and monitoring systems. In particular, the Agency should relate its data to data on effects collected by other agencies.*

We suggest that, among its other duties, staff in the proposed Office of Science direct such analyses (see Chapter 4). By identifying gaps and problems with monitoring programs, they can improve the quality of data and increase their usefulness for other purposes.

DISSEMINATION

Reducing Delays

The high cost associated with pollution and its control are reason enough to reduce the interval between collection of environmental data and their availability for analysis. At present, several years may elapse between collection and availability. In 1976, Congressional debates on revision of the Clean Air Act of 1970 were based, for the most part, on data that did not extend past 1973. The EPA National Human Tissue Monitoring Program, which studies levels of pesticides in body tissues, often requires years to enter the data on a computer unless there is a crisis, as in the cases of DDT, heptachlor-chlordane, and aldrin-dieldrin. Although 20,000 human adipose tissue samples were analyzed from 1967 to 1973, there had still been no formal publication of analyses of these data as late as 1974 (Spencer 1974). The soil, cropland, and estuarine pesticides monitoring programs are from one to four years behind in entering data on EPA computers. Analyses of data from the Community Health and Environmental Surveillance Study (CHESS), EPA's major program to study the health effects of air pollutants, were inordinately delayed. The first CHESS report (U.S. EPA 1974c), which contained an analysis of data collected during 1970-1971, did not appear until May 1974 and then contained only that part on sulfur dioxide and sulfates.

EPA is attempting to reduce these lengthy delays; a goal of six months has been set as the amount of time needed between collection of ambient air quality data by the states and its storage in EPA computers. The annual reports of CEQ and EPA can be more useful documents for Congressional and public evaluation of environmental policies, if they are based on more timely data and analysis. EPA should assure that its raw data and summaries of data are available to users within a year of their collection, or earlier if practicable. In addition, greater efforts should be made to inform potential users of the existence and usefulness of environmental data collections. CEQ's new computer system, User-Prompted Graphic Data Evaluation (UPGRADE), which can access and analyze a variety of environmental data of EPA and other federal agencies, seeks to broaden the community of users.

More Informative Annual Reports

An annual report should be timely; it should include concise summaries, interpretations of data, and explanations of the limitations of the data; and the report should identify its authors. We have examined several EPA reports with these characteristics in mind.

Timeliness Annual reports, to be more useful, must be timely. The public, Congress, and other groups depend on such summaries for understanding the progress of our environmental programs. And yet the first report on EPA's radiation program, which was established in 1970, did not appear until June 1976.

Concise Summaries Computer printouts should not be included if the same information appears in other, possibly more timely, EPA publications. Graphs and charts presenting information in a compact form should be more extensively used. EPA reports on ambient water quality (U.S. EPA 1975d) and on radiological effects (U.S. EPA 1976d) have been good in this regard. The EPA annual reports on ambient air quality (U.S. EPA 1973a, 1974d, 1976b), however, have too often neglected analyses, summaries, and informative graphs in favor of long lists of data from individual stations that are completely duplicated in more timely publications (U.S. EPA 1973b, 1974a, 1974b, 1975a). The most recent report (U.S. EPA 1976c) is an improvement; it contains some analyses and summaries without lists of data from individual stations.

Interpretations of Data If data on concentrations of pollutants are to be meaningful to a lay audience, they should be interpreted in comparison to standards or related to effects on health. In the radiation report (U.S. EPA 1976d), most values were given in the form of picocuries per liter, with no indication of how this might translate into more biologically meaningful units.

Limitations of Data   Biases in sampling, unreliable measurement methods, and uncertainties in dose-response relationships should be explained. In view of documented inaccuracies over the years of most of the EPA reference methods for air quality measurement, it would be appropriate for each annual report to explain problems with measurement methods and to indicate how reported values have been affected by these problems, especially when discontinuities are introduced by changes in the measurement process.

In addition, statistical measures of the variability of both the data and the summary measures should be reported. Data on environmental characteristics have many types of variability: temporal, spatial, and the variability of measurement both within and across laboratories. Measures of variability were not reported for most of the data collected by the EPA radiation program (U.S. EPA 1976d). On the other hand, the report on water quality (U.S. EPA 1975d) included measures of variability. These measures are important to help determine whether an observed large value of pollutant concentration may be the result of the vagaries of sampling or of other sources of variability. The water quality report also clearly explained that one could not extrapolate from the NWQSS sample of mostly larger and more heavily used rivers and streams to the entire nation.

Attribution   EPA should adopt a policy of identifying authors of its reports. The anonymous character of EPA publications, such as the *Monitoring and Air Quality Trends Report* (U.S. EPA 1974d, 1976b), means that those responsible are neither rewarded for a good job nor accountable for a bad one. The lack of recognition may discourage good prospective researchers from working at the Agency.

STATISTICAL RESOURCES OF EPA

Although the construction and interpretation of many of the statistics required by EPA's routine work call upon common sense qualities encouraged by scientific training, there are important classes of problems that require additional statistical insights and techniques. Deriving intelligible and useful relationships from data, drawing conclusions from processes being observed, and especially assessing the uncertainty of inferences, frequently require statistical insight coupled with experience in various statistical methods. Designing cost–effective monitoring networks, inferring the effects of pollutants on health, or providing environmental guidelines and standards that can withstand scientific and legal challenges also require a high level of statistical sophistication.

Furthermore, broad policy decisions and specific actions commonly depend on data processing and information handling systems that contain statistical components and that must serve the purposes of statistical analyses.

Perhaps the most important responsibility of administrators is to assess the value of their programs. Central to such assessments is an understanding of the quality of the work accomplished, of the reliability of the information provided, and of measures of effectiveness and cost. This understanding involves important statistical elements and requires skilled statistical judgment. It is relevant, therefore, to investigate the statistical resources of EPA and to assess them in relation to the Agency's responsibilities and needs. Similar investigations of EPA's resources in other professional fields would also be relevant, but EPA appears to appreciate the relevance of statistics less than it does that of many other fields.

REVIEW OF EPA STATISTICAL ACTIVITIES

In May 1974, Alvin L. Alm, EPA Assistant Administrator for Planning and Management, appointed an in-house ad hoc Statistics Review Committee to report to management about the Agency's performance and needs in statistical matters. We view this move as commendable. Independently, we examined the Agency from an external perspective. Both investigations have found the Agency unable to meet its statistical needs that derive from its ultimate objective of protecting the environment. The result of this inability has been a waste of resources and decreased efficiency in managing the environment.

In its investigation of the statistical activities of EPA, the ad hoc Statistics Review Committee studied EPA reports to Congress, sampled surveys and contracts sponsored by EPA, interviewed EPA managers, and questioned directors and professional statisticians at other federal agencies.[7]

The Review Committee examined 16 of 23 reports sent from the Agency to Congress. They found that 14 of the 16 reports "contained results which were based upon a substantial amount of mathematical and statistical analyses. The most prevalent types of analyses were trend and prediction, sampling, multifactor experimental design and modeling." Clearly, both statistical analysis and inference proved important in

[7]U.S. Environmental Protection Agency (1974) Draft report of the Statistics Review Committee to the Assistant Administrator for Planning and Management, October 11, 1974, David R. Monti, Chairman. Internal EPA Document.

communicating the accomplishments of the Agency to Congress and to the nation.

A random sample of 29 EPA surveys approved by the Office of Management and Budget was studied by the Review Committee. It determined that only 11 surveys were made with the help of a qualified statistician, no survey quoted the precision of estimates, only 7 stated hypotheses to be tested, only 9 ran a pretest, only 14 had a non-response mechanism, and only 3 had a respondent bias mechanism. Many surveys neglected to describe the method of sample collection; others used samples that were clearly too small (or perhaps too large).

Twelve hundred contracts were awarded by EPA in FY 1974. The Review Committee examined those contracts for which the funding exceeded $50,000. Of these, approximately 35 percent appeared to have a statistical orientation, based on their titles. A random sample of 26 of the statistically oriented contracts was chosen for further analysis, and the project officers were interviewed. "The results of the interviews showed, with some exceptions, that provisions for statistical design and application were not being provided for, either in-house or by the contractor . . . " and that " . . . project officers had no or very little understanding of statistics. . . . "[8] Evidently many experimental programs had both produced and analyzed data with only modest concern for statistical principles.

The Review Committee also held personal interviews with 54 top and middle managers in EPA and concluded "that most managers were well aware of their need for statistical expertise and were generally concerned with meeting these needs." There were, however, 14 situations in which the interviewers perceived an obvious need for statistical capability that was unsuspected by the interviewed manager. On some other occasions where a need was admitted on the part of the manager, no personnel were available to meet the need. Other managers felt that training in statistics would meet their needs, but the report fails to mention any evidence of such training. A few of the managers interviewed felt their needs could be met by hiring a consultant. To the outsider, it seems clear that many of the managers interviewed were naive about their statistical needs and responsibilities. Many did not—perhaps could not—know their needs because they lacked an understanding of the field of statistics.

To compare this situation at EPA with that in other agencies, the Review Committee also reviewed statistical activities at the National Bureau of Standards, the National Institutes of Health, and the Bureau of the Census. All these organizations had a central statistical group that included statisticians of national reputation.

[8]See note 7 above.

Finally, the Review Committee made case studies of: (a) pesticides enforcement, (b) water compliance and ambient stream monitoring, and (c) the 1974 National Water Quality Report to Congress. The pesticides study highlighted "the important role of and critical need for proper and defensible statistics in the legal issue of enforcement of pesticides in particular and other standards in general." The other case studies documented the pervasive need for good statistical data and practice in policy decisions and in the establishment of guidelines and standards.

The report of the Review Committee concluded that the use of statistics was a major activity of the Agency, that the level of statistical expertise within the Agency was low relative to its needs, and that the quality of statistical performance was frequently poor.

We made independent investigations of many of the Agency's published documents, the reports of its contractors, and its regulations and guidelines. In general, the level of statistical understanding demonstrated in these documents was meager. There were, however, some outstanding exceptions, among them the current reports on collaborative testing of analytical methods for measuring ambient air quality characteristics.

EPA AND THE LANGUAGE OF STATISTICS

A discouraging aspect of many EPA publications that employ statistics is the failure to use the language of statistics properly.[9] In some respects, statistics is a branch of applied mathematics, and at least as much care must be exercised in the use of statistical language as in the use of

---

[9]Repeated illustrations of the misuse of statistical language in the publications of EPA can be documented. Most common are fuzzy uses of the words "precision," "accuracy," and "confidence." For example, consider the description of the EPA reference method for the criteria air pollutants that appears in the *Federal Register* (U.S. EPA 1971) under the caption "Precision, Accuracy and Stability" for SO_2, we read: "Relative standard deviation at the 95 percent confidence level is 4.6 percent for the analytical procedure using standard samples." We can interpret "relative standard deviation" to mean the coefficient of variation. But the phrase "at the 95 percent confidence level" is undecipherable: too many interpretations are possible. In an attempt to unfold the meaning of this statement, we checked the literature cited in the *Federal Register* only to discover that the estimate of the "relative standard deviation" had been based on three observations and that there was no way to determine how the 95 percent statement was arrived at. The statistical statement in the *Federal Register* is not only unclear; it is based on sketchy information. Elsewhere in this same document, we find separate and different definitions of precision for each of the criteria air pollutants. Much of this carelessness in the use of statistical terminology was undoubtedly due to the haste with which regulations and reports were once written and to the obvious multiplicity of authorship. Unfortunately, other examples of this kind can be found in current issues of the *Federal Register*, as well as in recent publications from the Agency.

mathematical language. Indeed, greater care may be essential, since statistics often deals with uncertainty and inductive inference. In particular, the definition of terms must be explicit. The failure to be clear can not only confuse the reader; but, what is more serious, it can cause problems in the interpretation and enforcement of regulations.

EPA's use of statistical terms should reflect their careful definition. In particular, the phrasing of probability statements, especially those associated with confidence intervals and tests of hypotheses, should be carefully composed if they are to be correctly interpreted. Administrators expect reports to be written in English that is understandable. The same criterion should be applied when the language of statistics is employed. Good regulation, like good science, must strive for clarity.

Statistical terms and statements appearing in the official publications of EPA should be adequately checked to insure that only carefully defined statistical terms are used and that they are used properly.

EPA AND UNUSUAL STATISTICS

Statistics of unusual construction frequently occur in the Agency's publications.[10] The mathematical structure of common statistics, such as the average, range, sample variance, and coefficient of variation, has been extensively studied. As a result, probability statements and valid inferences, based upon their simple arithmetical forms and upon additional assumptions reasonably satisfied in practice, are possible. This ease of analysis and interpretation, however, is not the case for every statistic. The construction of statistics to quantify concepts, particularly in documents that carry the weight of law, must be carefully done. EPA regulations and guidelines in the *Federal Register* and official EPA documents should be reviewed to uncover instances of poorly designed statistics so that they may be corrected or revised.

---

[10]For example, the EPA standards of performance for new stationary sources are described in the *Federal Register* (U.S. EPA 1975f). On page 46265 under a discussion of sewage treatment plants, the concept "accuracy" is quantified by an unusual statistic. We read, "Accuracy is reported as the sum of the absolute value of the mean difference and 95 percent confidence interval of the differences expressed as a percentage of the mean reference method value." The mathematical and probabilistic characteristics of this statistic are unknown, and it is difficult to say whether any observed value is unusual or commonplace or to draw any inferences. In short, this statistic is not scientifically useful. Other unusual statistics, such as the "contribution error," and computation techniques appear in other EPA announcements in this same issue of the *Federal Register*.

EPA AND THE PROPER CHOICE OF STATISTICS

The Agency should pay more attention to the proper choice of statistics in monitoring. The Occupational Safety and Health Administration, for example, has recognized the need for a time-weighted measure of exposure for a regulation under which a worker may spend some time working at high ambient concentrations of certain substances, provided that sufficient time is also spent at low concentrations so that his total daily exposure remains within proper limits.[11] The importance of the proper choice of statistics is also apparent in studies of health effects. For example, a reported 24-hour average of sulfur dioxide is not as useful as more detailed measurements, since exposure at 0.5 ppm for one hour may be harmful. Information on different averaging times is available from hundreds of continuous sulfur dioxide monitors. When the objectives underlying the collection of data are clearly stated, both the amounts of data and the corresponding elucidating statistics can be determined. EPA should reexamine its choice of statistics with a view to choosing, where feasible, statistics more illuminating with regard to health and ecological effects.

APPLICATION OF STATISTICS TO ENVIRONMENTAL PROBLEMS

EPA recognizes its obligation to educate its personnel and that of the states, municipalities, and industry in the environmental arts and sciences, particularly in the practice of monitoring. The extensive list of publications emanating from EPA reflects this concern. To focus attention on statistical methods, several EPA documents are currently available or in preparation. The *Quality Assurance Handbook for Air Pollution Measurement Systems, Volume 1, Principles* (von Lehmden and Nelson 1976) is a primer on statistical terminology and procedure relevant to the measurement of air pollutants. The essence of the handbook is contained in its appendixes, where one objective is to

---

[11]For example, consider two statistics, the exponentially weighted moving average and the cumulative sum, and the different effects of CO and asbestos on the body. A spiked dose of heavy concentration of CO lasting a minute, when inhaled, will have immediate consequences. But after a time, during which the body has had an opportunity to "wash" the resulting carboxolhemoglobin from the blood, no long-range effect remains. Thus, a useful statistic for monitoring CO concentration might be the exponentially weighted moving average since this statistic gives less and less weight to events that have occurred distant in time. But asbestos (if it is of appropriate size and type) remains permanently within the human body, and its effect on the health of the recipient is thought to be persistent. Thus, an appropriate statistic to use in monitoring asbestos might be the cumulative sum, a statistic which gives historical data the same emphasis as recent data.

explain commonly used statistical terms and to show how various calculations are performed. Similar material appears in books on industrial quality control. On the whole, this information has been presented well. A similar but shorter document, *Handbook for Analytical Quality Control in Water and Wastewater Laboratories* (Ballinger et al. 1972), discusses statistical problems associated with water laboratory quality control.

Yet, a crucial question should be asked: is the information on statistical methods given in these primers sufficient for persons engaged in pollution measurement? We think the answer is, "No." The adaptation of statistical techniques to the problems of environmental monitoring involves more than a bare recounting of standard methods without any illustration or discussion of their purpose. We prefer an exposition of statistics specifically adapted to environmental practice, along with documents on the uses of statistics in environmental monitoring that emphasize case histories involving real data.

Many recent statistical developments can be of immediate value to the Agency. The innovative application of statistical tools awaits exposition by statisticians familiar with the problems of the environmental scientist.[12] Rapid progress could be catalyzed by holding frequent small colloquia at which environmental scientists from EPA and other agencies could meet with statisticians drawn from the Agency, universities, and industry. Special efforts should be made in collaboration with the statistical community to develop and adopt new statistical methodologies applicable to problems of environmental monitoring.

STATISTICIANS IN EPA

The EPA Statistics Review Committee identified a total of 51 professional mathematicians, mathematical statisticians, and survey statisticians within the Agency, by using civil service classifications (1520, 1529, 1530). More than two-thirds were in the Office of Research and Development. The report noted that " . . . EPA would need thirty additional statistical personnel to have the same ratio of staff to statistical budget as the HEW . . . " and that " . . . an additional staff of two hundred and fifty would be needed to match the Food and Drug Administration's ratio."

We reviewed a later listing, perhaps incomplete, of EPA employees with responsibility or interest in the uses of statistics (EPA Environmen-

---

[12]A paper by P.M. Berthouex, "Monitoring Sewage Treatment Plant Performance," illustrates what is possible. (Working paper prepared for the NRC Study Group on Environmental Monitoring [1976]. See Appendix F for availability of this manuscript.)

tal Statistics User's Guide mailing list, August 22, 1975). Of this list of approximately 100 individuals, only 16 could be identified as members of the major statistical societies. Of these 16, most were recent university graduates; and, for several of them, EPA represented their first professional work experience. There are too few who, through their publications, consulting, teaching experience, research, or participation in the activities of the statistical societies, could be considered senior or nationally known statisticians. The preponderance of statisticians on this list were in the Office of Research and Development, many in the Human Studies Laboratory, Biometry Branch, at Research Triangle Park. No single organizational structure exists for Agency statisticians or for closely associated professionals in operations research, computer methods, econometrics, or mathematics. Personnel with these skills are scattered throughout the Agency, and little commonality of interest has developed.

This evidence is not offered as criticism of the professional statisticians already working within EPA. It is offered because it demonstrates that: (a) the number of professional statisticians in the Agency is too small; (b) there is no professional focus of statisticians, and statistical expertise is scattered throughout the Agency; (c) responsibility for the establishment and maintenance of good statistical practices is uncoordinated; (d) no statistician within EPA has sufficient rank to influence Agency decisions or to delay them on the basis of statistical deficiency; and (e) no statistician or statistical group within the Agency can consider the whole range of statistical concerns related to environmental problems in order to decide where statistical expertise could be brought to bear most effectively or to serve as statistical advisor to the Agency's top management.

CONCLUSIONS AND RECOMMENDATIONS

We have emphasized only some of the deficiencies that exist in the statistical activities of the Agency. There is, in addition, a serious failure to use statistical methods in the design and analysis of many experiments and surveys. The use of appropriate statistical techniques in sampling could be considerably broadened. The adaptation of new statistical methodologies is sluggish. There is little support for research and development of statistical techniques applicable to the environmental sciences. Greater efforts are needed to acquaint the statistical fraternity with the data gathering and analysis problems of the Agency. And finally, the role of uncertainty is often poorly incorporated in the establishment of environmental guidelines and standards (see Appendix C).

We know it is easy to complain. We also recognize that the Agency, in its efforts to meet the objectives set for it by Congress, has often not had the resources of time or talent to do many things as well as it would have liked. But, on the basis of both the report of the Agency's in-house ad hoc Statistics Review Committee and our own independent investigation, it is clear that Agency leadership has not recognized the significance of EPA's statistical responsibilities. The leadership is aware of the need for the collection of data and the maintenance of data files; but, beyond such "data librarianship," little effort has been made to secure the needed advice of senior professionals in statistics. Statistical problems have been left almost exclusively to nonstatisticians. The Agency has staffed itself with many experienced professionals, but those statisticians it has hired are mostly young, and without the practical power to seriously influence decisions. The time is overdue for the Agency to recognize itself as a major user of statistical techniques and expositor of statistical information and analysis.

We believe that sound statistical practices in EPA can only be assured if there is in-house capacity equal to meeting its problems.

• *We recommend that EPA develop, particularly in its Office of Science, talent of sufficient quantity and character to meet its many statistical responsibilities and that the Agency establish at least one senior statistician to advise EPA management on the entire range of the Agency's statistical concerns.*

A good example is the Statistical Engineering Laboratory of the National Bureau of Standards.

REFERENCES

Ballinger, D.G., R.L. Booth, M.R. Midgett, R.C. Kroner, and J.K. Kopp (1972) Handbook for Analytical Quality Control in Water and Wastewater Laboratories. Analytical Quality Control Laboratory, National Environmental Research Center. Cincinnati, Ohio: U.S. Environmental Protection Agency.

Box, G.E.P. (1974) Statistics and the environment. Journal of the Washington Academy of Sciences 64(2):52-59.

Bromberg, S.M., B.I. Bennett, and T.A. Clark (1975) Survey of System Performance: Analysis of Simulated Ambient Carbon Monoxide Samples. Survey No. 2, August 1974. Quality Assurance Performance Surveys. Environmental Monitoring and Support Laboratory. Research Triangle Park, N.C.: U.S. Environmental Protection Agency.

Burton, C.S. and G.M. Hidy (1974) Regional Air Pollution Study Program Objectives and Plans. A Report by Rockwell International for the Air Monitoring Center. EPA 630/3-75-009. Washington, D.C.: U.S. Environmental Protection Agency; PB-247 769/3BE. Springfield, Va.: National Technical Information Service.

Hunter, J.S. (1977) Quality Assessment of Measurement Methods. Supplement I, Environmental Monitoring: Analytical Studies for the U.S. Environmental Protection Agency, Volume IV. Report of the Study Group on Environmental Monitoring. National Research Council, Committee on National Statistics, Assembly of Mathematical and Physical Sciences. Washington, D.C.: National Academy of Sciences.

Jurgens, R.B. and R.C. Rhodes (1975) Quality assurance and data validation for the regional air monitoring system of the St. Louis regional air pollution study. Pages 730-735, Proceedings of a Conference on Environmental Modeling and Simulation, April 19-22, 1976, Cincinnati, Ohio. Office of Research and Development, Environmental Monitoring and Support Laboratory, EPA-600/9-76-016. Research Triangle Park, N.C.: U.S. Environmental Protection Agency; PB-257 142. Springfield, Va.: National Technical Information Service.

Libster, L. (1976) Environmental Information Systems Directory: An Inventory of Environmental Systems. Management Information and Data Systems Division. Washington, D.C.: U.S. Environmental Protection Agency; PB 251 170/7BE. Springfield, Va.: National Technical Information Service.

Spencer, D.A. (1974) The National Pesticide Monitoring Program: An Overview of the First Ten Years of the Program's Operation. Washington, D.C.: National Agricultural Chemicals Association.

U.S. Environmental Protection Agency (1971) National Primary and Secondary Ambient Air Quality Standards 36 Fr 8186.

U.S. Environmental Protection Agency (1973a) Monitoring and Air Quality Trends Report, 1972. Monitoring and Data Analysis Division, EPA 450/1-73-004. Research Triangle Park, N.C.: U.S. Environmental Protection Agency; BP-234 445/5. Springfield, Va.: National Technical Information Service.

U.S. Environmental Protection Agency (1973b) The National Air Monitoring Program: Air Quality and Emissions Trends. Volume 1: Annual Report. Office of Air and Water Programs, EPA 450/1-73-001a. Research Triangle Park, N.C.: U.S. Environmental Protection Agency; PB-226 490/1. Springfield, Va.: National Technical Information Service.

U.S. Environmental Protection Agency (1973c) Water Programs: Guidelines establishing test procedures for analysis of pollutants. 38 FR 28757-29760.

U.S. Environmental Protection Agency (1974a) Air Quality Data. 1972 Annual Statistics. Office of Air Quality Planning and Standards, EPA 450/2-74-001. Research Triangle Park, N.C.: U.S. Environmental Protection Agency; PB-232 588/4. Springfield, Va.: National Technical Information Service.

U.S. Environmental Protection Agency (1974b) Air Quality Data. 1973 Annual Statistics. Office of Air Quality Planning and Standards, EPA 450/2-74-015. Research Triangle Park, N.C.: U.S. Environmental Protection Agency; PB-241 808/5BE. Springfield, Va.: National Technical Information Service.

U.S. Environmental Protection Agency (1974c) Health Consequences of Sulfur Oxides: A Report from CHESS, 1970-1971. Final Report. National Environmental Research Center, EPA 650/1-74-004. Research Triangle Park, N.C.: U.S. Environmental Protection Agency; PB-234 920/7. Springfield, Va.: National Technical Information Service.

U.S. Environmental Protection Agency (1974d) Monitoring and Air Quality Trends Report, 1973. Office of Air Quality Planning and Standards, EPA 450/1-74-007. Research Triangle Park, N.C.: U.S. Environmental Protection Agency; PB-240 484/6BE. Springfield, Va.: National Technical Information Service.

U.S. Environmental Protection Agency (1975a) Air Quality Data. 1974 First Quarter Statistics. Office of Air Quality Planning and Standards, EPA 450/2-75-002. Research

Triangle Park, N.C.: U.S. Environmental Protection Agency; PB-257 806/0BE. Springfield, Va.: National Technical Information Service.

U.S. Environmental Protection Agency (1975b) Environmental Radioactivity Laboratory Intercomparison Studies Program 1975. National Environmental Research Center, Technical Support Laboratory, Environmental Monitoring Series, EPA 680/4-75-002b. Las Vegas, Nev.: U.S. Environmental Protection Agency; PB-243 636/8BE. Springfield, Va.: National Technical Information Service.

U.S. Environmental Protection Agency (1975c) Minimal Requirements for a Water Quality Assurance Program. Office of Water and Hazardous Materials, EPA-440/9-75-010. Washington, D.C.: U.S. Environmental Protection Agency.

U.S. Environmental Protection Agency (1975d) National Water Quality Inventory—1975 Report to Congress. Washington, D.C.: U.S. Environmental Protection Agency.

U.S. Environmental Protection Agency (1975e) Radiation Quality Assurance Intercomparison Studies 1974-1975. Quality Assurance Branch, Environmental Monitoring and Support Laboratory, EPA 600/4-75-014. Las Vegas, Nev.: U.S. Environmental Protection Agency; PB-248 171/1BE. Springfield, Va.: National Technical Information Service.

U.S. Environmental Protection Agency (1975f) Standards of performance for new stationary sources: Emission monitoring requirements and revisions to performance testing methods. 40 FR 46250.

U.S. Environmental Protection Agency (1975g) Water Programs: National Interim Primary Drinking Water Regulations: 141.28 Approved laboratories. 40 FR 59573.

U.S. Environmental Protection Agency (1976a) Audit and Study of the RAMS/RAPS Programs and Preparation of a Quality Assurance Program for RAPS. EPA Contract No. 68-02-1772. Research Triangle Park, N.C.: U.S. Environmental Protection Agency.

U.S. Environmental Protection Agency (1976b) Monitoring and Air Quality Trends Report, 1974. Office of Air Quality Planning and Standards, EPA 450/1-76-001. Research Triangle Park, N.C.: U.S. Environmental Protection Agency; PB-252 269/6BE. Springfield, Va.: National Technical Information Service.

U.S. Environmental Protection Agency (1976c) National Air Quality and Emissions Trends Report, 1975. Office of Air Quality Planning and Standards, EPA 450/1-76-002. Research Triangle Park, N.C.: U.S. Environmental Protection Agency.

U.S. Environmental Protection Agency (1976d) Radiological Quality of the Environment. Office of Radiation Programs, EPA 520/1-76-010. Washington, D.C.: U.S. Environmental Protection Agency; PB-254 615/8BE. Springfield, Va.: National Technical Information Service.

von Lehmden, D.J. and C. Nelson (1976) Quality Assurance Handbook for Air Pollution Measurement Systems. Volume 1, Principles. Quality Assurance Branch, Environmental Monitoring and Support Laboratory, EPA 600/9-76-005, Research Triangle Park, N.C.: U.S. Environmental Protection Agency; PB-254 658/8BE. Springfield, Va.: National Technical Information Service.

4 Toward More Effective National Environmental Monitoring

NEED FOR AN EPA COMMITMENT TO SCIENTIFIC PRINCIPLES

Throughout this report, we have documented the need for better use of scientific principles in EPA's programs, in particular, in the design, operation, and evaluation of monitoring systems. At present, scientific expertise within EPA principally rests in the Office of Research and Development, which employs about 1000 scientists and engineers in its headquarters and 15 research laboratories. Within the Office of Research and Development is the Office of the Principal Science Advisor, composed of senior advisors on engineering and the physical sciences. In addition, the Agency has established an independent Science Advisory Board of about 350 members to advise EPA on its scientific policy. For specific advice on air and water monitoring, EPA has formed two ad hoc Standing Work Groups which report to the Deputy Administrator.

The current organization of scientific activities in the Agency, however, does not allow for the integration of scientific principles into EPA's operations. Valuable research is conducted or supported by the Agency, but it is insufficient and the results are inadequately applied to monitoring. Sound scientific principles should be incorporated into all EPA activities, not only into research and development.

In addition, EPA should establish programs to monitor not only for the control of pollution but also for the measurement of its effects and for

99

anticipation and discovery of environmental problems, so that effects of pollution can be at least diminished and, at best, prevented.

FRAGMENTATION OF MONITORING ACTIVITIES

Responsibilities for environmental monitoring are fragmented, and there is inadequate coordination among programs serving different purposes. Separate programs often exist where a single program could serve multiple needs. Little coordination exists for the monitoring of pollutants in different media, so that, for example, pollutants are measured in air that are not measured in water, soil, or food, and vice versa. Environmental characteristics are monitored independently: data on water pollution are collected that are not accompanied by data on flow, and air pollutants are measured that are not accompanied by information on important meteorologic and other characteristics and on concomitant pollutants that determine harmful effects.

Furthermore, there is inadequate coordination among federal, regional, state, and local agencies and even among EPA programs themselves. A result is that the synthesis of pollution data and the study of relationships between data on pollution and data on effects are hindered by incompatible methods of data collection and processing. Because knowledge from disparate scientific disciplines relevant to monitoring is not sufficiently integrated, many types of scientific expertise are absent from the design and evaluation of monitoring systems and the analysis of data.

Our case study of the Maumee "Estuary" (see Appendix B) illustrates some problems in coordination of monitoring activities. A variety of federal, state, and local agencies investigated pollution problems in the basin and recommended or ordered corrective actions. In addition, four agencies monitored water quality continuously. Many agencies had overlapping programs for collection and analysis of data; at least six had significant replications. Another equally serious problem is that the data, once collected, were not useful or available for analysis. Finally, the lack of a clear understanding of how the data were to be used—whether for baseline analysis, mass balance calculations, or hydrologic model formation—led to either insufficient or excessive data collection.

Our survey in Allegheny County,[1] on the other hand, offers an example of a wide variety of water quality monitoring efforts coordinated at the local level. The survey sought to identify organizations that were

[1]Rome, D.L. and I.L. Whitman (1977) A Case Study of Environmental Monitoring in Allegheny County, Pennsylvania. Working paper for the Study Group on Environmental Monitoring. (See Appendix F for information on its availability.)

monitoring in the region, to determine the extent of duplication and coordination of their activities, and to determine whether the needs of data users were being met. It identified 24 organizations carrying out monitoring activities and 33 using data from those activities. Most of the users were data collectors. The survey was not exhaustive; few industries, municipal facilities, or public utilities were contacted, although they collect extensive data that are not generally available to the public. Little duplication was found, even among the 13 organizations active in monitoring water quality. A local USGS office and the Ohio River Valley Water Sanitation Commission (ORSANCO) provided coordination for some activities. Use of the USGS Catalog of Information on Water Data (USGS 1973a, 1973b) and the EPA STORET data bank prevented duplicate monitoring for ambient water quality data. Many users or potential users of monitoring data, however, indicated that their data needs were not being satisfied. Missing were sufficient data on effects. Only three organizations monitored effects: the Game Commission, the local Agricultural Extension Service, and the County Coroner. Some users experienced difficulties in obtaining or understanding air quality data.

As discussed in Chapter 2, one reason for the fragmented nature of monitoring is that EPA does not provide objectives, priorities, criteria, and other policies of environmental monitoring in terms that are useful in the design and evaluation of monitoring systems. As a result, monitoring programs are designed with little or no assessment of their contribution to a national system or to the success of an overall national environmental program. We discussed the need for EPA to work collaboratively with federal, state, and local agencies in developing prototypes for monitoring networks, measurement methods, and data systems. EPA has also failed to provide adequate policies for developing an understanding of the natural environment and of the chronic effects of environmental contaminants on humans, animals, and plants. The absence of such policies has impeded the development of programs that are coordinated on a national scale.

CONSTRAINTS ON MONITORING IMPOSED BY CONGRESS

Legislation that requires monitoring has contributed to the fragmentation and poor design of our monitoring programs. Congress, frustrated by the lack of information on environmental degradation and its implications for economic, social, and other public policies, has frequently included specific requirements for reports on the nation's environmental programs in legislation, such as the Federal Water Pollution Control Act, the Safe

Drinking Water Act, and the Clean Air Act. Many of these requirements are so detailed that they prescribe, for all practical purposes, the design of environmental monitoring systems. The Federal Water Pollution Control Act includes 29 such requirements; the Safe Drinking Water Act, six; and the Clean Air Act, eight. Many additional reporting requirements are included in regulations and guidelines issued pursuant to these acts.

As an example, Section 305(b) of the Federal Water Pollution Control Act includes data collection and monitoring requirements with considerable specificity, such as an annual report including: (a) a description of the water quality of all navigable waters in each state, with appropriate supplemental descriptions; (b) an analysis of the extent to which all navigable waters provide for the protection and propagation of shellfish, fish, and wildlife and allow recreational activities in and on the water; (c) an analysis of the extent to which the elimination of the discharge of pollutants and the resulting quality of water will provide for the protection and propagation of a balanced population of shellfish, fish, and wildlife and allow for recreational activities; (d) an estimate of the environmental impact and the economic and social costs necessary to achieve this objective; and (e) a description of the nature and extent of nonpoint sources and suggested programs to control them.

Congress, by legislating specific requirements for information from monitoring programs, denies EPA sufficient flexibility to design and operate such programs. Ironically, the requirements for so many reports undermine the dictum in Section 101 of the Federal Water Pollution Control Act for the "drastic minimization of paperwork." The Administrator of EPA should be allowed discretion to design a nationwide system that meets the needs of Congress, EPA, and state and local environmental protection agencies at reasonable cost. Monitoring activities must constitute an effective national system that will provide a broad range of information concerning the state of the environment and the progress of environmental management programs. With flexibility, the EPA Administrator should be able to adjust the system to newer requirements, focus on specific problems, and assure the relevance, quality, and efficiency of this national system.

Although legislation imposes restrictive requirements on monitoring, the authorization for EPA to require monitoring is often broad and implied. We suggest to Congress and EPA that regulations requiring monitoring clearly state the purposes to be served by the data and encourage its efficienct collection. EPA guidelines and regulations in the *Code of Federal Regulations* should be audited to remove requirements for unnecessary data programs.

AN EPA OFFICE OF SCIENCE

The scientific problems in the administration of EPA's programs indicate the need for a comprehensive solution. We have important gaps in environmental monitoring and, at the same time, a proliferation of uncoordinated, inefficient, and inflexible monitoring programs that produce, at great expense, data of poor or unknown quality. We conclude that a central reason for these problems is that environmental sciencies in EPA lack leadership in positions that could influence monitoring. Although we document only the problems of EPA's application of science to monitoring programs, we believe that these problems may be symptomatic of EPA's application of science more generally.

We considered several methods for integrating scientific principles into EPA's guidance of environmental monitoring, including the creation of separate groups in EPA to provide expertise and leadership for four scientific activities relevant to monitoring: (1) design of monitoring networks; (2) the measurement process; (3) statistics; and (4) analysis. But the problems associated with EPA's use of science seem so pervasive that we were led to a more general proposal for a single organization within the Agency. Furthermore, all scientific activities of EPA could benefit from such an organization, whether or not their other problems of applying scientific principles are as serious as those affecting monitoring.

- *We recommend that, within the EPA Administrator's office, an Office of Science be established to exert scientific leadership in EPA, to aid its programs by better integration of scientific principles, and to improve the efficiency and usefulness of data collection by more scientific influence and direction. The head of the Office should be a senior scientist who would advise the Administrator on science policy and, together with the staff, provide a focus of professional talent in the environmental sciences.*

Whether or not this recommendation is adopted, the problem must somehow be addressed that, for lack of scientific leadership, scientific principles are not adequately applied to the design, operation, and evaluation of monitoring programs.

ORGANIZATIONAL FRAMEWORK

Because scientific guidance is necessary for all EPA's activities, the Office of Science should be part of the Administrator's Office. From this position, the advice, analyses, evaluations, designs, and prototypes of the Office of Science could be applied to Agency decision making and to all

Agency programs, especially those calling for data collection. An Office of Science should neither manage nor be managed by other EPA offices in order to shield it from preoccupation with the transient exigencies of managing pollution control programs and from the obligation to respond to every environmental crisis. The senior scientist heading the Office of Science should report directly to the Administrator. With the authority of the Administrator, the Office should influence and give direction to data collection.

ROLES AND DUTIES

We envision a number of different duties and roles for this Office of Science. Not all tasks could be done directly by its staff. For the study of special problems the office should be empowered to convene groups, some of which could report directly to the Administrator. We have arranged our suggestions concerning roles and duties under general categories.

Collection, Processing, and Analysis of Data

Problems with data collection and analysis and with data systems have been discussed at length. We propose that an Office of Science help solve the problems by adopting the following responsibilities:

• providing scientific objectives and criteria in clear operational terms for the design and evaluation of monitoring networks;
• collaborating with federal, state, and local agencies to develop prototype monitoring network designs;
• conducting reviews and evaluations, from time to time, of current and proposed data processing or information handling systems of the Agency in conjunction with their associated monitoring programs;
• providing review and guidance to help improve the compatibility of measurement methods and quality assurance for the measurement process;
• working with the scientific community to develop and evaluate monitoring network designs and methods of sampling, measurement, and analysis;
• providing expertise in statistics, identifying statistical needs within the Agency, reviewing and helping to formulate EPA regulations, and correcting poorly designed statistics; and

• determining that data meet their intended purposes efficiently and that they serve as many purposes as possible, particularly by shaping efforts for EPA to analyze its environmental data for various purposes such as measuring the progress of environmental programs, studying relationships between pollution and its effects, and evaluating national monitoring programs.

The costs of data collection and data systems are an integral aspect of most of these responsibilities.

Coordination of Monitoring Programs

There is no central office in EPA with overall responsibilities for monitoring (see Figure 4.1). Environmental Sciences Research Laboratories develop new measurement methods, Environmental Monitoring and Support Laboratories provide expertise for state and local agencies, and ad hoc work groups guide the design of national monitoring networks. The Office of Monitoring and Technical Support in the EPA Office of Research and Development provides for quality assurance and supports monitoring in other ways, but the Office does not guide routine monitoring and data handling operations. These responsibilities belong to various program offices for different media. Coordination of these fragmented responsibilities would be facilitated if EPA provided leadership, through a central office, to assure (a) that monitoring systems were designed for clearly defined purposes, (b) that broader monitoring policies were established related to taking care of the environment over the longer term, and (c) that monitoring programs were coordinated within EPA and among EPA, and other federal, state, and local agencies. (Later, we discuss special coordination needed among federal agencies.) An Office of Science should provide this type of leadership and advice. Measurements of substances in air, water, biota, and soil should be made and sufficient information collected so that they can be compared with one another. Data processing methods should be compatible, and definitions and protocols for sampling and measurement should be uniform. Mutual compatability of monitoring programs is essential if the programs are to function as a national system.

Review of Reporting Requirements

Unnecessary constraints on monitoring imposed by legislation and regulations should be removed. The staff of the Office of Science could be helpful with such a review.

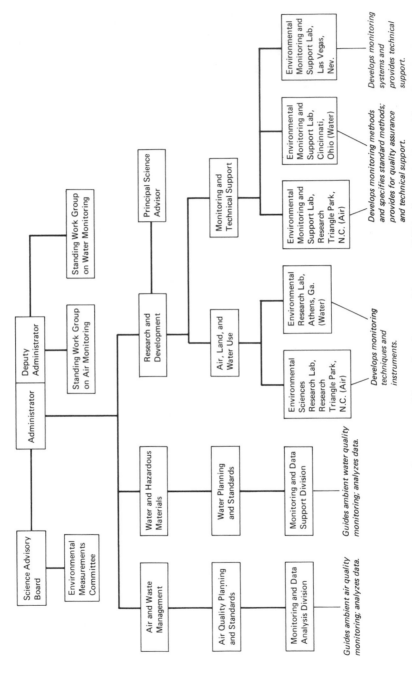

FIGURE 4.1 Some offices in the U.S. Environmental Protection Agency with responsibilities for monitoring ambient air and water quality (excluding effects monitoring).

- *We recommend that monitoring information and reporting requirements imposed by legislation and EPA regulations be reviewed and changes suggested in those that decrease the effectiveness of monitoring programs or impose unnecessary costs. EPA should conduct such a review cooperatively with federal, state, and local agencies.*

Scientific Review of EPA Research and Decisions

It is a common practice to send a research manuscript or proposal to other scientists for their commentary or approval before publication in a scientific journal or before research has begun. A reviewer often makes suggestions for improving a manuscript or proposal or may even recommend against publication or conduct of the research. An editor of a scientific journal typically sends a manuscript to several reviewers or referees. Some results of EPA and EPA-sponsored research are published in refereed scientific journals; but most appear in the form of EPA reports, which may have a greater impact on public policy than journal articles. These reports should be submitted to external scientific review by experts to validate and add credibility to the results of the research, to improve the quality of the research, to increase dissemination of the methods and results, and to provide greater interaction with the outside scientific community.

- *We recommend that EPA research reports, at least those that may have a major impact on public policy, receive external scientific review by experts prior to publication.*

In addition EPA should, whenever possible, see that designs for proposed research receive external scientific review before the Agency conducts or sponsors the research. The task of selecting some external reviewers might be assumed by the Office of Science. If time is not severely limited, EPA and EPA-sponsored research should be published in appropriate scientific journals where adequate review is assured. Even research published internally could be published in appropriate form in journals as well.

Most journals, however, will not publish extensive tabulations of data, and such printed tabulations are no longer the most appropriate way to publish them anyway. For this reason we suggest that EPA make the data from its research more easily available and, in the case of major environmental studies, encourage other researchers to further analyze raw data. Extensive data tabulations could be provided on computer tapes. Some EPA journals and reports, such as *Radiation Reports* and the

Pesticides Monitoring Journal, are valuable sources of data, which should continue to be published.

EPA's decision making would also benefit from scientific review. Prior to issuing regulations, EPA should publish the analyses upon which its decisions were based, including an adequate exposition of whatever physics, chemistry, and economics may be involved. Any deficiencies in analysis or data may be uncovered in this way, and monitoring programs and subsequent decisions may be improved.

Improving Cost–Effectiveness of Monitoring Programs

We suggest that the Office of Science also periodically reevaluate monitoring programs to improve their cost–effectiveness. Because of changes in both the environment and the methods of sampling it, relationships between cost and effectiveness of a monitoring system can change rapidly. A poorly sited station, discovery of a new pollutant, development of a new measurement method—these and other changing factors require continuing analysis to maintain cost–effectiveness.

Study of Long-term Monitoring Policies

There is no organization in EPA that has the time and mandate to set the Agency's long-term monitoring policies. Therefore, monitoring systems are either hastily assembled in response to separate pieces of legislation (such as the Clean Air Act and the Federal Water Pollution Control Act and their amendments) or they are never developed at all, as illustrated by EPA's neglect to monitor on a national basis some important air pollutants that are not regulated. The Office of Science should study long-term issues affecting monitoring, such as increased use of effects monitoring as opposed to ambient monitoring and alternative methods of environmental management.

A NATIONAL COMMITTEE ON ENVIRONMENTAL MONITORING

Problems with the coordination of monitoring activities extend beyond those previously discussed. There is also a lack of coordination among federal agencies. Data relevant to environmental management are collected by many federal agencies. Their efforts should be coordinated, particularly so that data on environmental quality can be related to data on health and ecological effects and so that EPA can monitor the responses of humans, animals, and plants to changes in environmental quality. We discussed in Chapter 3 the need to analyze relationships between environmental data and data on health and suggested some sources of data that could be further explored for this purpose.

An example of needed coordination can be found in the monitoring of heavy metals. Certain heavy metals are measured in human tissues and blood in the Health and Nutrition Examination Survey of NCHS; another set is measured in the Market Basket Survey of the Food and Drug Administration; others are measured in drinking water by some state agencies; and still others are measured in ambient air by some EPA monitoring stations and state agencies. Identification of the resulting gaps could improve monitoring systems to collect data concerning all of the important ways in which humans are exposed to pollutants.

Environmental data processing and information handling systems are another example of needed coordination. A 1974 GAO study (U.S. GAO 1974) identified over 300 such systems in the federal government, operated by 72 different offices. EPA led the list with 87 systems, followed by Interior with 61, Commerce with 39, and Agriculture with 33. The study showed that only 25 percent of EPA systems share data with other federal departments or agencies; between 52 percent and 82 percent of the systems in other agencies share data. The report indicated that managers of 151 environmental data systems expressed the need for an overall directory of such systems to identify existing sources of information, to reduce search time and number of referrals, and to prevent duplication in data collection. Several agencies have directories of their own data systems or referral centers for types of environmental data; but no central body exists for coordination of environmental data systems. Even within EPA, data systems proliferate without regard to other existing systems.

Another activity that could profit from coordination is the monitoring of the various media through which pollutants travel. Intensive multimedium studies of pollutants emitted to the atmosphere, discharged in streams, buried in the soil, leached by groundwater, and accumulated by animals and plants in the vicinity of industries would supplement our current knowledge based on data from fixed stations.

Coordination of data collection is needed to provide information to guide our environmental management policies. EPA alone, however, cannot provide this coordination. We see the need to establish a group to coordinate environmental monitoring activities among federal agencies, including those that collect data on health. This group, by working cooperatively with states and local agencies, could serve to make federal environmental monitoring programs part of a mutually compatible national system.

• *We recommend that a National Committee on Environmental Monitoring be established to coordinate federal environmental monitoring efforts.*

We suggest that the Committee be an interagency group with one federal agency responsible for convening the group and providing the secretariat. The Committee should include representatives from industry, state and local agencies, and professional scientific groups. It should have a small interdisciplinary scientific staff and should report to Congress and the heads of relevant agencies at least every two years.

The Committee should assume the following responsibilities, among others:

• encouraging studies that relate environmental data to medical, energy, biological, ecological, and socioeconomic data: for example, the Committee could bring together scientists of various agencies to assure that sufficient data are collected in ways appropriate for such studies;

• finding ways to insure that measurements taken by one Agency will serve the needs of others: for example, the Committee could suggest that data sets be coded with the same geographical index to facilitate useful comparisons;

• finding ways to insure that monitoring programs carried out by different agencies are comprehensive but do not duplicate the work performed by others: for example, the Committee could clarify potentially overlapping responsibilities for monitoring by federal agencies;

• suggesting ways to improve communication among producers and consumers of environmental data and scientists and engineers working on problems of environmental monitoring: for example, the Committee might call research conferences, set up interagency committees, or suggest other means to encourage work on newly perceived monitoring problems or data requirements; and

• identifying long-term environmental problems that affect many different agencies (such as the impact of new technologies) to anticipate problems and facilitate coordinated studies.

These responsibilities are only some that might be handled by the Committee. Efforts to solve the problems should not be delayed until it is formed. If our recommendation for a Committee is not adopted, the problems will need to be addressed in other ways.

Each monitoring system represents only a piece of a large and complex puzzle. The puzzle, if completely put together, would show the relationships between sources of residuals and ambient environmental quality and between substances encountered in the environment and their effects on human health, plant growth, abundance of fish and wildlife, and other aspects of human well-being. But putting the puzzle together requires synthesizing and coordinating abilities of a high order. EPA alone cannot solve this complex problem: the Agency will need help from all parties concerned.

REFERENCES

U.S. General Accounting Office (1974) Federal Environmental Data Systems. Report to the Subcommittee on Fisheries and Wildlife Conservation and the Environment, Committee on Merchant Marine and Fisheries, U.S. House of Representatives, by Comptroller General of the United States. Washington, D.C.: U.S. General Accounting Office.

U.S. Geological Survey (1973a) Catalog of Information on Water Data. Water Resources Region 02 (Mid Atlantic). Office of Water Data Coordination. 1972 edition. Washington, D.C.: U.S. Geological Survey.

U.S. Geological Survey (1973b) Catalog of Information on Water Data. Water Resources Region 05 (Ohio). Office of Water Data Coordination, 1972 edition. Washington, D.C.: U.S. Geological Survey.

APPENDIX
A

Monitoring for Genetic Effects in Man

James V. Neel[1]

INTRODUCTION

The possible genetic effects of environmental pollutants first attracted widespread attention in the wake of World War II, when the potential genetic effects of fallout from the testing of atomic weapons created great concern among scientists. The result has been a series of national and international efforts to assess the situation (NRC 1956, 1972; UN 1958, 1962, 1966). These assessments revealed substantial uncertainties about the possible effects of low-level chronic radiation exposures that might result from fallout (now diminished because of the decrease in weapons testing) or from radiation resulting from peaceful uses of the atom, including diagnostic X-rays. The uncertainties continue to create difficulties for cost–benefit analyses.

More recently, however, the earlier concerns over the possible genetic effects from exposure to man-made sources of radiation have received relatively less attention because of the recognition of the extent of chemical pollutants in the environment, and their possible genetic implications (Committee 17 1975). There are even greater uncertainties here than in the area of radiation exposure. In the case of the latter, information about gonad exposure from radiation is reasonably accurate (Klement et al. 1972), and calculations can be made, albeit within a wide

[1]The author is grateful for the comments of James F. Crow, University of Wisconsin, Madison; H. Eldon Sutton, The University of Texas at Austin; and Friedrich Vogel, Institute for Anthropology and Human Genetics of the University of Heidelberg.

113

range of uncertainty, concerning effects on future generations and even the cost to future generations in dollars per rem unit of exposure (NRC 1972, Grahn 1976).

The case for the ubiquity of the exposure of human populations to potentially mutagenic chemical pollutants is easily made. The chemicals include such agents as: the fungicide, captan; the plant-growth inhibitor, maleic hydrazide; the food preservatives, sodium nitrite and sodium nitrate; certain of the streptomyces-derived antibiotics; various insect chemosterilants, such as triethylene phosphoramide and triethylene melamine; the benzopyrene found in smog; and a variety of alkylating agents. The latter, such as ethylenimine, dimethyl and diethyl sulfate, methyl and ethyl methanesulfonate, and others, are widely used in industry in methylating or ethylating phenols, amines, and other compounds. These chemicals reach our respiratory and alimentary tracts in minute amounts, by way of air and water pollution, food preservatives, and residual pesticides and medications. The precise level of exposure however, and the extent to which the mutagenic chemicals reach gonadal tissue remain largely unknown.

With respect to the issue of radiation effects, during the past 30 years extensive tests have been performed on an appropriate experimental animal (the mouse), and the findings can within limits be extrapolated to man. In contrast, no such extensive work is currently being done for potential chemical mutagens. Furthermore, the chemical pollutants raise an additional investigative problem not associated with radiation. There are so many potential chemical mutagens in the environment, that while the concentration of any one may be at a "safe level," their cumulative effect may well be significant, especially if they act synergistically.

THE EFFECTS OF CHANGES IN MUTATION RATES

We are concerned about the possibility of increased mutation rates for two reasons. First, it is the intuitive belief of many geneticists that the mutation rate of a species, as established through the operation of natural selection, should be close to optimum for that species. Second, we have seen from experimental demonstrations, especially in *Drosophila*, that most induced mutations have deleterious effects.

The latter concept—the generally deleterious effects of mutation—has recently been challenged by the discovery of large amounts of previously concealed genetic variability, revealed by biochemical techniques. This finding has led to the suggestion that the "new" alleles resulting from mutation which are retained in populations are often neutral with respect to natural selection. It has also been shown that mice, rats, and swine receiving relatively large doses of radiation over a series of generations do not appear to show net dominantly-inherited deleterious effects. This suggests, among possible explanations, that an unexpectedly "efficient" elimination of new mutants occurs, or that current estimates of induced mutations in *Drosophila* are not applicable to mammals (Green 1968, King 1968). Finally, under certain circumstances, irradiation over a series of generations actually seems to improve the fitness of *Drosophila* populations (Wallace 1968). This demonstration does not contravene the principle that a significant proportion of induced mutations are deleterious, but rather emphasizes the importance of understanding the selective process in long-range predictions. All these developments have introduced a large measure of caution into predictions of the impact of increased mutation rates on populations, but they do not lessen the need for an evaluation of the situation.

PUBLIC PROTECTION THROUGH SCREENING

Each year, a variety of new chemical products is introduced into industry or released on the market. There are elaborate regulations for screening these products for carcinogenicity. No less stringent regulations are indicated with respect to the mutagenicity of these compounds. Indeed, in view of the close empirical relationship being developed between mutagenicity and carcinogenicity, a screening for mutagenicity may in fact serve as a screening for carcinogenicity.

The technique of screening for mutagenicity is now reasonably well established; a review of the techniques can be found in Hollaender (1971-73). In general, a three tier test system is recommended. The first level involves tests with bacteria, for which Ames has developed especially suitable strains (Ames et al. 1975; McCann et al. 1975; McCann and Ames 1976, In Press). The second level of the tier involves the use of special strains of *Drosophila*. The third level involves cultured mammalian cells. At each level, a decision is made as to whether the indications of mutagenicity (and carcinogenicity or other somatic effects) outweigh the potential value of the agent. If there remains doubt after these screens—if the agent appears of great potential value but troublesome questions about mutagenicity persist—then the final screen tests the effectiveness of the agent in producing germinal mutations in a mammal, the house mouse. Some would advocate earlier introduction of an in vivo mammalian test system (by far the most expensive of the approaches) because of the demonstrated extent to which intermediary metabolites, rather than the administered chemical, are the real mutagens, and the inability to predict for a mammalian system just what those metabolites might be.

Observance of this tier test system would greatly aid in the identification of mutagens that may have serious consequences for man. However, many agents that individually pass the screening tests may cumulate in the body, perhaps with synergistic effects, causing significantly increased mutation rates. Furthermore, laboratory experience has increased the possibility that mutagens which in experimental systems are only moderately effective may be converted within the body by man's intermediary metabolism into much more effective mutagens, a possibility that infra-human screening systems cannot exclude (see especially Huberman et al. 1976).

PUBLIC PROTECTION THROUGH MONITORING

Geneticists have been actively directing public attention to uncertainties in knowledge about environmental mutagens, and the public has been attentive. Thus, one reason for challenging the use of nuclear energy is the possible genetic consequences of increased exposure to radiation. Similar considerations are emerging in efforts to carry out cost–benefit analyses for other types of energy-generating procedures. Given the magnitude of the issues involved, it is time to undertake a vigorous exploration of the most appropriate ways to monitor human populations.

APPROACHES TO MONITORING HUMAN POPULATIONS

There are three principal approaches to detecting an increased germinal mutation rate in a human population.

"Population Characteristics" Approach

The "population characteristics" approach uses changes in such demographic events as frequency of stillbirths, mean birthweight, frequency of congenital defect, sex ratio, death rates during the early years of life, and physical growth and development during infancy and childhood as indications of an increase (or decrease) in mutation rates. The argument that an increased mutation rate should be reflected in these indicators is simple and sound, but the relationship between any given change in the indicator and the underlying change in mutation rate is not clear. Furthermore, we know that all these indicators are influenced by many exogenous factors operating on both mother and child. A suitable control population must be available. Establishing such a control group, however, becomes increasingly difficult in view of the great heterogeneity in human communities.

To date, the principal search for evidence of an increased human mutation rate used this approach to study children born to the survivors of the atomic bombings at Hiroshima and Nagasaki. It was felt that the population base was not adequate for the "sentinel phenotypes" approach (see below), and science had not yet provided us with the tools for the study of biochemical or chromosomal mutations (see below). The study, its findings, and problems in interpreting the results have been presented in several summary publications (Neel and Schull 1956, Neel 1963, Neel et al. 1974). This approach, undertaken a generation ago, has been superseded by recent scientific developments.

"Sentinel Phenotypes" Approach

The "sentinel phenotypes" approach monitors a defined population (or contrasts two suitable populations) for changes in the rate of occurrence of isolated cases (within the family) of certain phenotypes likely to have resulted from a dominant mutation in a germ cell. Table A.1 lists many of the phenotypes that have previously been used to estimate mutation rates in man, as well as the estimates so derived (Vogel and Rathenberg 1975).

There has been considerable discussion as to whether or not these rates are representative of all human genes. It has been suggested, most strongly by Stevenson and Kerr (1967) and Cavalli-Sforza and Bodmer (1971), that since the very rare inherited phenotypes are not selected for studies of mutation rate, the existing estimates generally involve the more mutable genetic loci. From a careful survey of sex-linked traits, Stevenson and Kerr suggest that average rates for traits such as this are more nearly 1×10^{-6}/gene/generation. Undoubtedly, mutation rate studies have selected some phenotypes which appear relatively frequently through mutation, but on a more theoretical level it can be argued that all loci have similar mutation rates if all changes in the genetic material could be taken into consideration. For some, any change in the gene product has a phenotypic counterpart, whereas other loci are much less "sensitive" (Neel 1957). If this is so, the element of bias in the selection of traits for such studies does not mean that the existing estimates are as unrepresentative of the total mutational spectrum per locus as they may first appear. However, for monitoring purposes, it matters little whether these rates are typical, providing that the relative response of specific loci to various mutagens is similar to that of the loci in general.

There are other problems, theoretical and practical, in the use of sentinel phenotypes. On the theoretical side, isolated cases of some of these phenotypes could represent non-genetic developmental accidents, could be the result of somatic mutation, or could be due to recessive inheritance. Mutation at any one of several different loci may result in clinically indistinguishable phenotypes. In laboratory jargon, these are

TABLE A.1 Selected "Classical" Mutation Rates for Human Genes

Trait	Population Examined	Mutation Rate	Number of Mutants/ 10^6 Gametes
A. Autosomal Mutations			
1. Achondroplasia	Denmark	1×10^{-5}	10
	Northern Ireland	1.3×10^{-5}	13
	Germany (Reg. Bez. Münster)	$6-9 \times 10^{-6}$	6–9
2. Aniridia	Denmark	$2.9(-5) \times 10^{-6}$	2.9(–5)
	Michigan (USA)	2.6×10^{-6}	2.6
3. Dystrophia myotonica	Northern Ireland	8×10^{-6}	8
	Switzerland	1.1×10^{-5}	11
4. Retinoblastoma	England, Michigan (USA), Switzerland, Germany	$6-7 \times 10^{-6}$	6–7
	Hungary	6×10^{-6}	6
	The Netherlands	1.23×10^{-5}	12.3
	Japan	8×10^{-6}	8
	France	5×10^{-6}	5
5. Acrocephalosyndactyly (Apert's syndrome)	England	3×10^{-6}	3
	Germany (Reg. Bez. Münster)	4×10^{-6}	4
6. Osteogenesis imperfecta	Sweden	$0.7-1.3 \times 10^{-5}$	7–13
	Germany (Reg. Bez. Münster)	1.0×10^{-5}	10
7. Tuberous sclerosis (epiloia)	Oxford Regional Hospital Board Area (GB)	1.05×10^{-5}	10.5
	Chinese	6×10^{-6}	6
8. Neurofibromatosis	Michigan (USA)	1×10^{-4}	100
	Moscow (USSR)	$4.4-4.9 \times 10^{-5}$	44–49
9. Polyposis intestini	Michigan (USA)	1.3×10^{-5}	13
10. Marfan's syndrome	Northern Ireland	$4.2-5.8 \times 10^{-6}$	4.2–5.8
11. Polycystic disease of the kidneys	Denmark	$6.5-12 \times 10^{-5}$	65–120
12. Diaphyseal aclasis (multiple exostoses)	Germany (Reg. Bez. Münster)	$6.3-9.1 \times 10^{-6}$	6.3–9.1
13. von Hippel-Lindau syndrome	Germany	1.8×10^{-7}	0.18

B. Sex-linked Recessive Mutations

14. Hemophilia	Denmark	3.2×10^{-5}	32
	Switzerland	2.2×10^{-5}	22
	Germany (Reg. Bez. Münster)	2.3×10^{-5}	23
Hemophilia A	Germany (Hamburg)	5.7×10^{-5}	57
	Finland	3.2×10^{-5}	32
Hemophilia B	Germany (Hamburg)	3×10^{-6}	3
	Finland	2×10^{-6}	2
15. Duchenne-type muscular dystrophy	Utah (USA)	9.5×10^{-5}	95
	Northumberland and Durham (GB)	4.3×10^{-5}	43
	Südbaden (Germany)	4.8×10^{-5}	48
	Northern Ireland	6.0×10^{-5}	60
	Leeds (GB)	4.7×10^{-5}	47
	Wisconsin (USA)	9.2×10^{-5}	92
	Bern (Switzerland)	7.3×10^{-5}	73
	Fukuoko (Japan)	6.5×10^{-5}	65
	Northeast England (GB)	10.5×10^{-5}	105
	Warsaw (Poland)	4.6×10^{-5}	46
16. Incontinentia pigmenti (Bloch-Sulzberger)	Germany (Reg. Bez. Münster)	$0.6\text{–}2.0 \times 10^{-5}$	6–20
17. Oculofaciodigital syndrome (OFD)	Germany (Reg. Bez. Münster)	5×10^{-6}	5

not "clean" systems. On the practical side, the chief problems are selecting traits for which there are minimal diagnostic problems in the very young, and establishing a suitable registration system in a sufficiently large study population.

Let us consider the size of the population that must be under intensive surveillance for these defects to detect a 50 percent increase in mutation rates in a single year. This seems to be the maximum increase that should be permitted to go undetected. Let us assume that those phenotypes listed in Table A.1 that would be suitable for such a study (and possibly several others not yet recognized) collectively amount to 50 appearances per 100,000 births. We do not have a "true" rate, but an estimate. Our problem is to determine the size of the population necessary to demonstrate, at the 0.05 or 0.01 level of significance, that an increase in mutation rates has occurred. In other words, if an increase from 50 appearances per 100,000 births to 75 per 100,000 has in fact occurred, how many births must be monitored to be confident of detecting an increase at the indicated statistical level?

The computation must take into account type II errors, i.e., the probability of rejecting a real change in rate of the magnitude indicated. The figures shown in Table A.2 are based on a one-tailed probability test. If we accept a β (type II) value of 0.20, it requires two samples of approximately 121,000 births at the 0.05 level, or two samples of 196,000 at the 0.01 level. A crude birth rate of 20 per 1000 population requires a study population of 6,050,000 or 9,800,000, depending on the desired statistical level, if one wishes to place the detection system on a year-to-year basis. The size of the population whose births are to be followed can be proportionately reduced if the monitoring is placed on a two- or three-year, or even longer cycle.

Biochemical and/or Chromosomal Approach

Traditionally, a distinction has been made between two types of germinal mutations: "point" (in the strict sense involving alterations in the genetic code) and "chromosomal" (usually thought of as involving chromosomal additions, subtractions, or structural alterations detectable with the light microscope). Recent and pending developments in human cytogenetics and human biochemical genetics raise the possibility of examining mutation in man at both these levels, on a scale and with a precision unthinkable a few years ago.

The evidence for "point" mutations has for the most part been derived from studies at the level of gross organismic phenotypes, the genes for which could be localized to specific regions in the chromosomes by suitable breeding tests. Our ability to study "point" mutation in man with

TABLE A.2   The Sample Sizes Necessary to Detect an Increase in
Certain Sentinel Phenotypes[a]

Value of α	Value of β		
	0.10	0.20	0.49
0.05	167,172	120,688	54,035
0.01	254,101	195,911	108,136

[a]From an observed 50 per 100,000 births to 75 per 100,000 births, at the indicated probability levels for Type I (α) and Type II (β) errors. The t-values are based on one-tailed probability distributions.

SOURCE: Neel, J. V. (1972) Mutagenic Effects of Environmental Contaminants, edited by H. E. Sutton and M. I. Harris. New York:Academic Press.

conventional genetic techniques remains seriously restricted by the paucity of suitable chromosomal markers, the small size of the kindreds generally available for study, and the length of the human life cycle. Additional difficulties have been mentioned in the discussion of "sentinel phenotypes," which, until proven otherwise, are assumed to result from point mutations.

Recent advances in our ability to isolate and characterize a wide variety of human proteins, coupled with knowledge of the genetic code and its relationship to amino acid sequences, seem to permit us to circumvent many of the previous difficulties, and to approach the subject of mutation in man at a new and more precise level. In short, it is now possible to examine a representative series of proteins in placental cord blood or blood specimens from children, for variation in serum or erythrocyte proteins. When a variant is encountered, it is possible to determine by suitable family studies whether it was inherited from one parent or the other, or whether both parents are normal and the variant presumably resulted from mutation. The choice of material is dictated solely by technical considerations, thus reducing or eliminating the possible bias discussed in reference to mutability. Similarly, the problem of phenocopies and recessive inheritance contributing to the trait under consideration, and so distorting mutation rate estimates, is negligible in this approach. It seems clear that this approach, although still untried, theoretically offers a more precise evaluation of changes in mutation rates than do the other two.

The technology in this field is evolving rapidly. This is not the place for detailed considerations, but attention is particularly directed to the emergence of microtechniques which use blood specimens absorbed on filter paper, and of alternatives to electrophoresis for the detection of abnormal proteins through screening. Indeed, if there were a decision to undertake on a large scale a monitoring program employing these technologies, pilot studies employing a variety of methodologies seem to be indicated.

By past standards, full implementation of the biochemical/chromosomal approach will require a major effort, both for original screenings and for follow-up studies to separate mutants from nonmutants. Monitoring can be based either on the contrast of the progeny of "high risk" with the progeny of "control" groups (from which, presumably, extrapolation can be made to the general population), or on a continuous monitoring system in which time trends are studied in a "typical" population. The latter approach, while administratively simpler, requires more observations. For instance, let us assume that spontaneous mutation results in detectable changes in a protein at a rate of 0.5×10^{-5}/locus/generation. Let us assume that we can monitor for 20 different proteins (see Table A.3) and that we wish to be able to detect a 50 percent increase in the frequency of mutations at the 0.05 or 0.01 signifcance level. We wish to detect an increase from an estimated 20 per 100,000 births to 30 per 100,000 births, employing a one-tailed significance test. If we accept a type II (β) error of 0.20, it will require, at the 0.05 level, studying two samples of 313,000 persons each for all 20 proteins, or, at the 0.01 level, 508,000 person determinations. Even with automation, 313,000 person determinations represents the annual output of *at least* 200 technicians and 25 supervisory scientists, perhaps double that number. However, in many discussions of monitoring, consideration is given to three- or five-year cycles with a corresponding reduction in annual personnel requirements. Furthermore, other technologies now under consideration could considerably reduce the personnel needs. A type II error of 0.20 is fairly restrictive, but the calculation has been made at this level on the assumption that one wants to be reasonably certain of not missing a real effect. If contrasts are to be made annually, employing cord blood, it will be necessary to have a base population (crude birth rate of 20 per 1000) of approximately 15,650,000 or 25,400,000 persons. The necessary numbers for different values of β are given in Table A.4.

It is apparent that a large laboratory operation as well as a formidable "collecting net" must be organized. The task would presumably be shared by a number of centers. The decision to undertake a study of this magnitude requires careful consideration. However, having emphasized the risks to society of increased mutation rates, geneticists can scarcely draw back from the effort to assign this undertaking a proper priority among society's needs.

TABLE A.3 A Partial List of Proteins of the Erythrocyte and Blood Serum Which Can Now Be Satisfactorily Screened for Electrophoretic Variants[a]

BLOOD SERUM	ERYTHROCYTE (continued)
Albumin	Glucose-6-phosphate dehydrogenase
α_1-Antitrypsin	Glutamate dehydrogenase
Ceruloplasmin	Glutamic pyruvate transaminase
Haptoglobin	Glutathione reductase
Pseudocholinesterase	Glyceraldehyde-3-phosphate
Transferrins	dehydrogenase
	Glyoxalate
ERYTHROCYTE	Hemoglobin A
Acid phosphatase	Hemoglobin A_2
Adenosine deaminase	Hexokinase
Adenylate kinase	Isocitrate dehydrogenase
Aldolase	Lactate dehydrogenase
Carbonic anhydrase I	Malic dehydrogenase
Carbonic anhydrase II	Nucleoside phosphorylase
Catalase	Peptidase A
Diaphorase	Peptidase B
Diphosphoglycerate mutase	6-Phosphoglucose dehydrogenase
Enolase	Phosphoglucomutase
Esterase A	Phosphohexose isomerase
Esterase D	Pyruvate kinase
Galactose-1-phosphate uridyl	Triose phosphate isomerase
transferase	

[a]Relatively little has thus far been done with the proteins of the leucocyte; this appears to be an important field for investigation.

TABLE A.4 The Sample Sizes Necessary to Detect an Increase in Certain Biochemical Mutants[a]

	Value of β		
Value of α	0.10	0.20	0.51
0.05	434,012	313,329	135,265
0.01	659,695	508,603	270,445

[a]From an observed frequency of 20 per 100,000 births to 30 per 100,000 births, at the indicated probability levels for Type I (α) and Type II (β) errors. The t-values are based on one-tailed probability distributions.

SOURCE: Neel, J. V. (1972) Mutagenic Effects of Environmental Contaminants, edited by H. E. Sutton and M. I. Harris. New York: Academic Press.

In any monitoring scheme employing cord blood samples, serious consideration must be given to the inclusion of chromosomal studies. The same blood sample drawn for the above mentioned purposes could be examined for evidence of cytological damage to the chromosomes of the individual concerned. Here too, the technology is evolving rapidly; it may be possible to automate a large part of the work currently associated with karyotyping. About 1 in 200 persons possesses a gross chromosomal abnormality, approximately half having arisen from a chromosomal mutation in the preceding generation. In addition, newer techniques of studying chromosome fine structure in man reveal that approximately 2 percent of the population carry intrachromosomal inversions. These could be the selectively neutral survivors of a much larger group; little is known about their frequency at birth.

Both the "sentinel phenotype" and the biochemical/chromosomal approaches require that, in any instance of apparent mutation, the most complete genetic studies possible must be performed, using the now standard panel of genetic markers, to ensure that parentage is as stated. With respect to the biochemical/chromosomal approach, mislabelling of samples in the course of laboratory studies is an additional possibility for "false mutation," but it can be detected with the same accuracy as a true discrepancy between legal and biological parentage. In either case, there will be a small residuum of apparent mutations for which the true explanation is undetected mislabelling in the laboratory or true parentage discrepancies. These will dilute the study of mutation rates, but their frequency can be computed and due allowance made in any properly conducted study.

It is possible that a program which monitors cord blood specimens for mutation rates can also be useful in the early detection of disease. Unfortunately, phenylketonuria, the most striking example of success in the early detection of inherited disease, and several other rarer examples of serious inherited diseases, cannot currently be detected by the analysis of blood samples until the child is at least 3 to 4 days old. There are, however, other disease states, such as the congenital inability to synthesize thyroglobulin, which can be diagnosed at birth. Deficiencies of several of the enzymes listed in Table A.3 are also associated with disease states. The possible usefulness of such a program in the early detection of disease should not be lightly put aside.

MONITORING MUTATION RATES IN SOMATIC CELLS

Mutation is not restricted to germ cells—those destined to become spermatozoa or eggs—but occurs, as far as is now known, in all the diverse cells of the body. Because of the ease of "biopsy," the leucocytes and erythrocytes found in the blood are particularly favorable cell types in which to study somatic cell (non-sex cell) mutation. As now visualized, studies of mutation in these cells would concentrate on the detection of cells one or more of whose attributes (proteins) differed from those of the vast majority of other cells. Leucocytes are preferable to erythrocytes for this purpose because in theory if an abnormal leucocyte of the proper type is detected by methods that do not kill the cell, it can be propagated by cell culture techniques and the genetic nature of the change verified. In contrast, human erythrocytes cannot be propagated, because they are enucleate; therefore, crucial genetic tests cannot be performed.

Monitoring programs based on somatic cells theoretically have much to recommend them over programs based on germinal cells. A single blood sample permits the examination of many millions of cells for mutations. Thus, monitoring a relatively few individuals in key industrial installations should easily yield as many tests of mutation as the large programs described above. Unfortunately, techniques for monitoring individual somatic cells in vivo are lagging far behind those for testing individuals for the presence of a germinal mutation which affects protein structure.

The one major objection to reliance on such an approach at the present time—aside from the fact that the techniques are not yet at hand—is that the "conversion factor" to relate somatic cell mutation rates to germinal cell rates is completely unknown. The circumstances of blood cell proliferation are sufficiently different from those of germ cell proliferation (and passage to the next generation) that somatic cell mutation rates could be substantially higher (or lower) than germ cell rates.

Because of the theoretical attractiveness of this approach (and its relative inexpensiveness), it would be highly desirable to include somatic cell studies, as these become feasible, in any program monitoring for germ cell rates. Furthermore, once the necessary "conversion factor" has been established, it should be possible to substitute in whole or part the far less expensive somatic cell approach for the large-scale population studies described above.

SOME ADMINISTRATIVE CONSIDERATIONS

Arguments over the pros and cons of various approaches to monitoring rapidly become too technical for a general treatment such as this (cf. Neel 1972). We suggest that if the appropriate administrative body be receptive to the suggestion concerning human population monitoring, a conference should be convened specifically to develop the most satisfactory methodologies currently feasible. The agenda for such a conference should include the following considerations:

Sample Selection. Two alternatives must be considered. The first is an ongoing system with an established cycle (3 to 5 years), where mutation rates are followed in a sample of children born to "typical Americans," and particular attention paid to time trends. The other alternative is to compare mutation rates in children thought to be at high risk, because of the occupation of their parents, with rates in a suitable control group of children. The two sampling methods will provide different types of information; the first, the changing risks for U.S. children as a group; the second, the maximum risk to which any group of children is exposed.

Location of Monitoring Sites. Because of problems in transporting samples, and the need for a comprehensive understanding of the situation in the United States, it seems clear that the work should be divided among strategically located laboratories. The questions are how many, and where should they be located?

Blood Sampling. The principal sampling possibilities are (a) to draw umbilical cord blood samples from the placentae of newborn infants, or (b) to obtain samples from children of various ages. The method of cord blood samples has much to recommend it, but there may be instances where a group of children of various ages, thought to be at high risk, should be examined.

Invasion of Privacy. Informed parental consent procedures must be followed, involving an explanation of the purposes of the research and the possible risks to subjects before they consent to participate. What is the appropriate explanation? In the case of an apparent mutant, appropriate studies must be performed to ensure that the legal parents are, in fact, the biological parents; how best to maintain the necessary confidentiality? What are the rights of access of subjects to a file such as this? The broader issue here—certain, in view of current trends, to receive scrutiny in due time—is the extent to which the government (assuming any monitoring program would be government-sponsored) is entitled to unearth "sensitive" facts concerning its citizens, facts kept confidential by every means possible in the interests of protecting these same citizens from noxious agents.

The Cost of Monitoring. It is difficult to put an accurate price on a program involving sentinel phenotypes or on one involving protein indicators plus chromosomal damage. The former is highly influenced by the structure of medical practice, the requirements for the reporting of disease, and the ease of collation of information—factors that are always changing. The latter program involves a rapidly evolving technology. It seems likely that the advisability of pilot studies on the cost of the different approaches would be an important item for any conference.

With respect to monitoring for sentinel phenotypes, it is suggested that monitoring in such a way as to detect a 50 percent increase in mutation at the 5 percent level, with a type II error of 0.20 (successive samples of 127,000 births each), would now cost approximately $5,000,000 to $6,000,000 per sample (excluding overhead or indirect cost). If the monitoring were on a five-year cycle, the cost would be $1,000,000 per year.

For the biochemical approach, monitoring successive samples of 313,000 births for 20 proteins, with the same precision, would cost approximately $9,000,000 to $10,000,000 per sample (excluding indirect costs). On a five-year cycle, the cost comes to roughly $2,000,000 per year. This estimate is based on the current state of the art in protein electrophoresis, with each protein studied separately. Developments under consideration might substantially reduce costs.

Interpretation of Data. In discussions of this topic, concern is often expressed that a study which failed to yield statistically significant findings would be interpreted as "negative" and result in false reassurance. This danger can be averted by clear recognition that there is no such thing as a negative outcome in this type of investigation. Rather, the data should be used to set upper limits, with specified probabilities, on the magnitude of the effect that might go undetected. In other words, we might not be able to demonstrate a statistically significant increase in a sample of appropriate size, but we could exclude the possibility that the mutation rate had increased by 50 percent or more. The exact level at which that exclusion is to be set must be discussed.

Identification of Responsible Mutagens. Given an increase in mutation rates from chemical agents, the formidable task remains of identifying the responsible agent or agents from among the many possible mutagens. We may never be able to solve the problem by direct observation of human populations; but on the basis of experiments with laboratory mammals, we may attempt to reduce exposure to the most potent mutagens. There thus emerges an interplay between monitoring programs and laboratory experimentation. The studies of mutation rates in somatic cells could play an important role in this respect. If, in the face of a rising germinal cell mutation rate, a particular group with an unusually high exposure to a potential mutagen exhibited a high somatic mutation rate, this exposure would certainly come under suspicion as contributing to the increased germinal rate. This suspicion would exist even if the exact conversion rate for somatic cell rates to germ cell rates had not been established. Whether or not action based on somatic cell rates had identified the cause of the increased germ cell rate would become apparent with subsequent monitoring.

The necessary decisions regarding permissible exposures will probably never be based on genetic considerations alone, but also on knowledge of the somatic effects, with both the genetic and somatic effects balanced against the benefits to society from continued—although, it is to be hoped, temporary—use of the agent. A conference would do well to address itself to this decision-making process.

REFERENCES

Ames, B.N., J. McCann, and E. Yamasaki (1975) Methods for detecting carcinogens and mutagens with the *Salmonella*/mammalian-microsome mutagenicity test. Mutation Research 31:347-364.

Cavalli-Sforza, L.L. and W.F. Bodmer (1971) The Genetics of Human Populations. San Francisco: W.H. Freeman and Co.

Committee 17 of the Environmental Mutagen Society (1975) Environmental mutagenic hazards. Science 187:503-514.

Grahn, D. (1976) Cost–benefit as weighted on genetic scales. Pages 371-384, Energy and the Environment: Cost–Benefit Analysis, edited by R.A. Karane and K.V. Morgan. New York: Pergamon Press.

Green, E.L. (1968) Reproductive fitness of descendents of mice exposed to spermatogonial irradiation. Radiation Research 35(2):263-281.

Hollaender, A., ed. (1971-1973) Chemical Mutagens: Principles and Methods for their Detection. 3 Volumes. New York: Plenum Press.

Huberman, E., L. Sachs, S.K. Yang, and H.V. Gelboin (1976) Identification of mutagenic metabolities of benzo[a]pyrene in mammalian cells. Proceedings of the National Academy of Sciences 73(2):607-611.

King, J.L. (1968) Dominant radiation effects on mouse populations. Genetics 58(4):625-631.

Klement, A.W., Jr., C.R. Miller, R.P. Minx, and B. Shleien (1972) Estimates of Ionizing Radiation Doses in the United States, 1960-2000. Division of Criteria and Standards, Office of Radiation Programs, ORP/CSD 72-1. Rockville, Md.: U.S. Environmental Protection Agency; PB-220 534. Springfield, Va.: National Technical Information Service.

McCann, J., E. Choi, E. Yamasaki, and B.N. Ames (1975) Detection of carcinogens as mutagens in the *Salmonella*/microsome test: Assay of 300 chemicals. Proceedings of the National Academy of Sciences U.S.A. 72(12):5135-5139.

McCann, J. and B.N. Ames (1976) Detection of carcinogens as mutagens in the *Salmonella*/microsome test: Assay of 300 Chemicals: Discussion. Proceedings of the National Academy of Sciences U.S.A. 73(3):950-954.

McCann, J. and B.N. Ames (In Press) The *Salmonella*/Microsome Mutagenicity Test: Predictive Value for Animal Carcinogenicity. Origins of Human Cancer. New York: Cold Spring Harbor Laboratory.

National Research Council (1956) The Biological Effects of Atomic Radiation. A Report to the Public. Washington, D.C.: National Academy of Sciences.

National Research Council (1972) The Effects on Populations of Exposure to Low Levels of Ionizing Radiation. Report of the Advisory Committee on the Biological Effects of Ionizing Radiation. Washington, D.C.: National Academy of Sciences.

Neel, J.V. (1957) Some problems in the estimation of spontaneous mutation rates in animals and man. Pages 139-150, Effects of Radiation on Human Heredity, Report for a Study Group convened by WHO. Geneva: World Health Organization.

Neel, J.V. (1963) Changing Perspectives on the Genetic Effects of Radiation. Springfield, Ill.: C.C. Thomas.

Neel, J.V. (1972) The detection of increased mutation rates in human populations. Pages 99-119, Mutagenic Effects of Environmental Contaminants, edited by H.E. Sutton and M.I. Harris. New York: Academic Press.

Neel, J.V. and W.J. Schull (1956) The Effect of Exposure to the Atomic Bombs on Pregnancy Termination in Hiroshima and Nagasaki. National Research Council, Publication No. 461. Washington, D.C.: National Academy of Sciences.

Neel, J.V., H. Kato, and W.J. Schull (1974) Mortality in the children of atomic bomb survivors and controls. Genetics 76(2):311-326.

Stevenson, A.C. and C.B. Kerr (1967) On the distributions of frequencies of mutation to genes determining harmful traits in man. Mutation Research 4(3):339-352.

United Nations (1958) Report of the United Nations Scientific Committee on the Effects of Atomic Radiation. General Assembly Official Records: Thirteenth Session, Supplement No. 17 (A/3838). New York: United Nations.

United Nations (1962) Report of the United Nations Scientific Committee on the Effects of Atomic Radiation. General Assembly Official Records: Seventeenth Session, Supplement No. 16 (A/5216). New York: United Nations.

United Nations (1966) Report of the United Nations Scientific Committee on the Effects of Atomic Radiation. General Assembly Official Records: Twenty-first Session, Supplement No. 14 (A/6314). New York: United Nations.

Vogel, F. and R. Rathenberg (1975) Spontaneous mutation in man. Pages 223-318, Advances in Human Genetics, Volume 5, edited by H. Harris and K. Hirschhorn. New York: Plenum Press.

Wallace, B. (1968) Topics in Population Genetics. New York: W.W. Norton.

The Maumee Estuary:
A Case Study[1]

Michael Shapiro *and* Myron Fiering

It would seem axiomatic that the type of monitoring data collected depends on how the data will be used. Yet some environmental management problems are sufficiently complex that one can not know at the outset the extent of the analysis that will be necessary to solve the problem. For example, can the problems in a given river basin be solved through the information provided by baseline data, or are the problems so complex that solution will depend on additional data for use in complicated hydrologic modeling? Is a long-term monitoring network as effective as periodic intensive surveys would be?

In an effort to answer some of these questions, the Study Group undertook a case study of the Maumee "estuary," an area with long-standing pollution problems and an extensive data base, to see if the data had affected water quality control decisions. This paper is an abridged version of that case study.

PHYSICAL CHARACTERISTICS

The Maumee River Basin encompasses about 6600 square miles of land, three-quarters of which is in the northwestern part of the State of Ohio. The geological and hydrological characteristics of the area combined with its intensive agriculture and significant concentrations of heavy

[1]Shapiro, M. and M.B. Fiering (1976) Maumee River Case Study. The manuscript upon which this abridged version is based may be examined through arrangements with the archivist of the National Academy of Sciences, Washington, D.C.

industry and urban population have created water quality problems throughout the basin. However, this report focuses on issues relating to the "estuary" in the lower reach of the Maumee River, the 15 mile segment through which the river discharges into Lake Erie. The problematic manner in which water quality data have been applied to water quality management decisions in the Maumee "estuary" makes this area particularly suitable for a case study.

The physical characteristics of Lake Erie greatly affect the Maumee "estuary" and Maumee Bay. Because of Lake Erie's long narrow shape, winds parallel to the major axis of the lake have an important impact on the dynamics of water movement. When winds blow from the northeast, the water levels rise in the western portion of the lake and drop in the east, forming a hydraulic gradient to balance the shearing forces of the wind. Southwest winds (the predominant direction in the region) cause the opposite effect. This phenomenon has caused water levels between the east and west shores to vary as much as 14 feet. When the wind blows steadily from the northeast or southwest, and then suddenly changes direction, an oscillation or seiche is formed. The changing levels in the lake affect the Maumee in much the same way that changing tides influence ocean estuaries; the net flow direction is not always outward.

Under normal conditions the tidal effect is beneficial for water quality in the "estuary." During flow reversals higher quality lake water dilutes the pollutants in the "estuary," while during low lake levels the Maumee is flushed. However, wind-driven changes occur less regularly than ordinary tidal effects. Lake level and wind pattern can combine to cause pollutants to build up in the "estuary," with water neither entering nor leaving, much like an inversion episode in air pollution. Such a problem has not occurred in recent years because of the generally high lake levels.

WASTEWATER DISCHARGES

Toledo is the commercial and industrial center of the region. In 1970 its population was 384,015, and an additional 100,000 people lived in Lucas County outside the city limits. The major portion of Toledo is served by the city's municipal wastewater treatment plant located about a half mile from the mouth of the Maumee, on the west bank of the river. Toledo draws its water from Lake Erie, not the river, so that discharges from the plant, which amount to about 100 cfs in dry weather, are net additions to the Maumee and significant portions of the total flow during low-flow periods. The plant is the largest point source on the Maumee, receiving the wastes of about 500,000 people and a number of large industries. Two smaller treatment plants are located further upstream on the Maumee "estuary," and other small plants are on Swan Creek which flows through Toledo just north of the Maumee, discharging into the latter five miles from its mouth.

One significant problem with Toldeo's municipal sewage system is that many of the wastes never reach the plant. Like many older urban areas the city is served by a combined sewer system. When stormwater flows exceed the capacity of the interceptors or treatment plant, regulators in the pipes open, diverting waste directly into adjacent waterways. In addition many of the regulators have functioned improperly, allowing wastes to discharge directly into the waters even during dry weather. These problems have been particularly severe for the interceptors running along Swan Creek and along the Ottawa River (also called Tenmile Creek) which flows north of Swan Creek and discharges into Maumee Bay.

As a result of the agricultural, municipal, and industrial impacts, and the hydrologic regime, water quality in the Maumee "estuary" is severely degraded. This is evident by its physical appearance, its smell during warm weather, and by consistent violations of the coliform and dissolved oxygen standards set by the Ohio Environmental Protection Agency (OEPA). OEPA has classified the "estuary" as "appropriate for warm water fisheries, for primary contact recreation, for processing by conventional treatment into public, industrial, and agricultural water supplies . . . " (Ohio Environmental Protection Agency 1975). The OEPA standards require that dissolved oxygen never be less than 4.0 mg/l and that for flows greater than the minimum average seven consecutive day low flow (MA7CD10), dissolved oxygen shall not be less than a daily average of 5.0 mg/l. The standards further require that the fecal coliform count not exceed 200 per 10 ml as a 30-day geometric mean based on not less than 5 samples or 400 per 100 ml in more than 10 percent of all samples during a 30-day average.

DATA COLLECTION EFFORTS IN THE MAUMEE

Many state, federal, and local agencies have investigated the pollution problems of the Maumee. As early as 1950, the Ohio Department of Health conducted an extensive survey, and in the early 1960s the Cleveland Office of the Federal Water Pollution Control Administration (FWPCA) did another thorough study. Currently there are three monitoring stations collecting data: one, at Waterville, operated since 1966 by the United States Geological Survey (USGS) and two operated since 1973 by the Ohio Environmental Protection Agency. The FWPCA and the USGS discontinued use of three additional monitoring stations. Since 1966, the Toledo Pollution Control Agency (TPCA) has been sampling at dozens of locations. Furthermore, monthly grab samples are taken both upstream and downstream from the city's treatment plant by the Toledo Division of Water Reclamation.

Of the four purposes for collecting ambient data—to establish base information and time trends, to measure compliance, to calibrate models, and to perform basic research—the first two can be considered explicit objectives of the data collection efforts on the Maumee. The data collection efforts were not designed for model calibration although the basic data have been used for this purpose. Most important, none of the data collection efforts were designed to establish a "mass balance" for the important fluxes in the system and, *partially as a consequence*, none of the programs took into account the hydraulics of the Maumee "estuary."

USES OF THE MONITORING DATA IN PLANNING AND MANAGEMENT

Under the provisions of section 303(E) of the 1972 amendments to the Federal Water Pollution Control Act (PL 92-500), the OEPA began preparation of a plan for the Maumee River Basin. As a new agency, with relatively little federal guidance, the OEPA understandably had difficulties developing a plan, and, in fact, a final report has not yet been issued. However, draft versions of the waste load allocation section of this report were available as early as 1974. This section of the report designated stream segments as either "effluent limited" or "water quality limited" in accord with federal requirements. The distinction is an important one. In effluent-limited reaches, water quality standards can be met by application of secondary treatment for municipal wastes, while in water quality limited reaches, higher and more expensive levels of treatment are required. The segment designated Maumee River IV, which included the Maumee from Waterville to the mouth, was classified as effluent limited. Swan Creek was designated as water quality limited. The methodology employed to make these designations was apparently a version of the Streeter-Phelps model for stream quality. Parameters of the model were not calibrated to water quality data, and the Maumee River IV segment was treated in the same fashion as other streams, using an MA7CD10 flow value of 71.7 cfs from the Waterville flow data. No mention was made of the river's estuarine behavior in this segment or of the major pollution contribution from Toledo's faulty regulators.

This omission was interesting because OEPA was well aware of the problem. In fact, Toledo had been ordered to have a monitoring system for the sewer regulators under construction by December 1972. But by 1974 the project was still under study. In that year, Region V of EPA began a program to assess the progress made by the states in implementing PL 92-500. A consulting firm, Enviro-Control of Rockville, Maryland, was hired to do a study of the lower Maumee. This study later received additional support from the Toledo Metropolitan Area Council of Governments under its 208 grant.

The results of this study came to be known as the "Horowitz Report" (Horowitz et al. 1975). Had EPA been looking for a way to stimulate action at the state and local level, it could not have made a more effective choice. Horowitz et al. disapproved of many aspects of the monitoring and enforcement program, and their criticisms were hard to ignore. In their evaluation, they noted:

. . . None of the routine monitoring programs around Toledo . . . produces valid data on water quality. None of the fixed point sampling stations . . . can provide adequate data on waters which are subject to vertical and horizontal stratification. Too many samples were taken near the shore and near the water surface, where boundary layer effects distort the sample. . . . The sampling apparatus is commonly inadequate. . . . Sample storage and preservation are often suspect; moreover, storage times are much too long in some of the laboratories. Few of the analytical laboratories pay sufficient attention to quality control . . . (Horowitz et al. 1975:3).

These various programs lead independent lives, and most of the agencies are only dimly aware of the others' existence. No one tries to coordinate sampling schedules, to standardize analytical procedures, to split samples for analysis, to pool resources, to share the cost of decent surveying equipment or even to inform OEPA of WQS violations (Horowitz et al. 1975:33).

. . . Sampling schemes must pay due attention to three major features of estuarine behavior: stratification, flow reversals, and irregular times of passage. Virtually all the data which have been amassed by the routine monitoring programs in the Toledo area should be dismissed for this reason alone (Horowitz et al. 1975:129).

Other points stressed by Horowitz et al. in their criticisms include the poorly functioning sewer regulators, the large contribution of organic sediments and nutrients from agricultural activities and the poor performance of Toledo's new secondary treatment plant. OEPA policy was criticized on a broad range of issues:

The DO standard specifies an absolute minimum as well as a daily average. Nowhere is one told where these measurements are to be taken (Horowitz et al. 1975:24).

It is curious that one set of standards is applied to waters as diverse as the estuary (which never contains less than billions of gallons of water) . . . to suburban Swan Creek and Tenmile Creek [Ottawa River] (whose dry weather flow is scarcely more than a trickle) . . . (Horowitz et al. 1975:27).

It is remarkable, then, that the OEPA's waste load allocation is so riddled with unknowns . . . . Many entries that aren't UK are wrong. . . . The most curious feature of this wasteload report is its hydraulic inappropriateness: the lower Maumee is treated as though it were a free flowing stream . . . (Horowitz et al. 1975:38).

Given the lack of reliable information on the dynamics of the "estuary," and the difficulties in the data and applicable standards, Horowitz et al. made short-term recommendations:

Far too much money is spent on technically deficient sampling and water-quality analysis. The bubbling sludge beds, leaky sewers, and gagging miasmas can be far more easily and cheaply detected by the unaided eye and nose than by the suspect methods of scientism run amuck. The two principal violations of WQS, low DO and high fecal coliform densities, occur just where anyone with normal vision and olfaction would think: near the sludge beds and dribbling sewers in downtown Toledo and near the STP. . . . The pollution problems have long been evident. The cures are the obvious ones: upgrade the sewers to eliminate the sludge beds and improve STP performances. . . . Until these persistent problems have been cured, there is no reason to spend another dollar on routine water quality monitoring (Horowitz et al. 1975:4).

With decent improvements in Toledo's sewers and STP effluent, the lower Maumee should be able to meet all the standards that have been established; the sole exception is the thermal effluent from Toledo's Edison Acme plant, whose effects extend beyond the current definition of a mixing zone (Horowitz et al. 1975:8).

To provide for rational long-range allocation of waste loads, Horowitz et al. recommended that a detailed investigation of the estuarine hydraulics and sediment dynamics be undertaken over a two-year period.

DEVELOPMENTS SINCE 1975

The extent to which the Horowitz report has contributed to the recent flurry of pollution control activity in Toledo is hard to determine at this point. A Toledo official[2] stated that pollution control agencies were aware of the issues raised in the report before the study was begun and that facilities planning (discussed below) was already underway. He claimed that Horowitz et al. "ran around and listened to old wives' tales" and never spoke with anyone at a decision-making level. The official did feel that the publicity generated by the report helped in getting support for necessary projects. John Adams, of the Toledo Metropolitan Area Council of Governments (TMACOG), who was listed as a co-author of the Horowitz report, had a somewhat different view of its usefulness. He

[2]The presentation in the remainder of this review is based upon telephone conversations with individuals in state and local agencies and consultants to the agencies.

felt that Horowitz had made significant contributions by calling attention to the inappropriateness of the MA7CD10 flow for the "estuary," by emphasizing the complex hydrology of the "estuary," and by highlighting the role of the leaky sewers.

Toledo's Division of Water Reclamation is currently completing a facilities planning study in accordance with Section 201 of PL 92-500. The study, which has taken two years, covers the Maumee "estuary," Swan Creek, and the Ottawa River and deals directly with the problems of the interceptor sewers. In attempting to identify the effects of point sources and sewer discharges upon water quality, the Division's consultants chose not to develop a complex hydrologic model of the "estuary," but rather to work with a more aggregate model. EPA's SWMM model was used to model the sewer system, but the water quality segment of the model was not used. The procedures employed were outlined briefly by Dr. George Kunkle of Earthview, Inc. Unfortunately, documentation of the analysis was not available in time for the preparation of this paper.

It was determined, through statistical analysis of the data obtained from a stage gauge at the mouth of the Maumee, that over a 30-day period the effects of flow reversal and flushing roughly cancelled each other out. Therefore the method of analysis that was chosen consisted of the establishment of monthly mass balances for the three bodies of water and for selected water quality parameters. Measured changes at gauging stations, point sources, and sewer overflows would be used as input and output. As part of this analysis a monitoring program for the sewers was instituted and new water quality sampling in the Maumee "estuary" undertaken. In the case of BOD, the mass balance was used to determine the BOD accumulation in the river segment over the averaging period. The accumulated BOD was converted to ultimate oxygen demand and the latter correlated with average dissolved oxygen concentrations in the segment. This correlation was the basis for predicting dissolved oxygen concentrations resulting from various control measures. However, this method predicts average monthly dissolved oxygen concentrations, while the state standards refer to daily averages. Currently, the only way to cope with this disparity is to build a safety factor into the monthly average. Presumably such a factor could be based upon a statistical analysis of the relationship between average monthly and minimum average daily flows.

Although new water quality measurements were taken during this study, the consultants had to rely heavily upon the TPCA records, at least for the Swan Creek and the Ottawa River studies. Kunkle disagreed with Horowitz's negative assessment of these data and considered the overall consistency of the TPCA data acceptable. Believing that the Maumee has been over sampled, he suggested the most effective strategy for the future would be to limit sampling to intensive studies conducted at five-year intervals. He also thought that the simple aggregate model was adequate for the purposes of decision making, and that a detailed hydrologic study of the type suggested by Horowitz was unnecessary (for decision making) at the present time.

As part of the 201 study, Toledo has installed the long-awaited telemetering system at 30 overflow points to monitor the performance of the sewer regulators. If this system, in conjunction with improved maintenance, eliminates the dry weather discharges from the interceptors, the consultants estimate that there will be a 50 percent reduction in the total BOD load of sewer discharges. Elimination of the other half, which is due to wet weather overflows, will be much more difficult and expensive. All the usual methods for control of these overflows are being considered: in-line and off-line storage, settling or screening systems, and so forth. The final decision will be a major test of the value of modeling and data collection to Toledo's pollution control program.

CONCLUSIONS

1. If the purpose of monitoring is to develop an environmental baseline or to trigger a more precise measurement program for enforcement proceedings, the current Maumee program (and any similar or equivalently comprehensive programs) is acceptable. If the purpose is to perform a consistent mass balance, a number of important assumptions must be made to use the existing level of data; this level would be inadequate if sensitivity analysis were to show that design decisions are even moderately sensitive to water quality characteristics.

2. A major problem in the Maumee is storm-water management. If the new sewer regulators function properly, the best information that could be derived from a continuing program would be a functional relationship between DO and storm-water control. Horowitz recommends a model to solve for the details of such a relationship. There is a substantial amount of experience in developing hydraulic models of the sort recommended by Horowitz, but little to suggest that a reliable model can be formulated for the Maumee. If the estuarine hydraulics could be modeled, then a more intensive water quality program would be required to calibrate the model. In other words, the current data base is too extensive for monitoring, and not extensive enough for calculating system parameters and using models for water quality management. However, caution must be used not to overestimate the ability of a complicated model to produce dramatically and reliably better results.

3. If the dynamic "estuary" model is to help monitor and evaluate the performance of the Toledo sewage treatment plant, a data base covering tributary flows, total discharge, and other large-scale features of the hydraulic regime is necessary to assure consistency and continuity. If the (smaller) tributary plants are to be evaluated, gauge measurements would suffice. The closeness of the Toledo plant to the mouth of the Maumee makes it difficult to model all the relevant hydrologic and hydraulic processes that affect plant performance.

4. Evaluations of this sort are an essential part of monitoring. This examination of the past data program in relation to the Maumee's problems leads to the following conclusion about the future course of the data program in that area. Many of the relevant decisions can be drawn from long-term averages (for which acceptable results can often be obtained through mass balances deduced from a modest analytical framework) requiring no further data collection or modeling. Where water quality processes are under study, short-term intensive programs are indicated, to be repeated after several years. This suggests that the Maumee data program, as elsewhere, may be planned about a set of observations for mass balances, supplemented by periodic short-term intensive programs. A coherent program developed along these lines could be no more costly than the present replicative observations which merely confirm what is already known.

REFERENCES

Horowitz, J., J.R. Adams, and L.A. Bazel (1975) Water Pollution Investigation: Maumee River and Toledo Area. Prepared in cooperation with Toledo Metropolitan Area Council of Governments for the U.S. Environmental Protection Agency by Enviro Control, Inc. EPA 905/9-74-018. Washington, D.C.: U.S. Environmental Protection Agency; PB-242 287/1BE. Springfield, Va.: National Technical Information Service.
Ohio Environmental Protection Agency (1975) Maumee River Basin 303[E] Planning Report. Columbus, Ohio: Ohio Environmental Protection Agency.

C Incorporating Uncertainty into Environmental Regulations

J. Stuart Hunter

ESTABLISHING WATER STANDARDS

The establishment of environmental guidelines and standards continues to be a major activity of EPA. For example, twenty-seven industrial categories are listed in the Federal Water Pollution Control Act Amendments of 1972 (PL 92-500) and these have been partitioned into some 500 subcategories. For each subcategory, major pollutants have been identified, and for each major pollutant, emission standards have been established based upon (a) the best practical control technology currently available (BPT), and (b) the best available technology economically achievable (BAT). Additional standards governing new source performances have also been promulgated. The law mandates that all industries will meet the BPT standards by July 1, 1977, and the BAT standards by July 1, 1983. Further, under PL 92-500, it is illegal to discharge pollutants into the nation's waters without a NPDES (National Pollutant Discharge Elimination System) permit. By September 1975, 63,000 permits had been requested and 44,000 permits granted.

In establishing the requirements of an NPDES permit, industries within a subcategory were asked to submit relevant data and information to the Agency. The Agency frequently augmented these data with their own special investigations and sampling programs. The Agency also prepared a "Development Document" containing these data plus information on the age and size of the industrial facilities, descriptions of the manufacturing processes, manpower requirements, climatic conditions, types and amounts of pollutants, treatability of pollutants and other economic information, all with the purpose of identifying the best industrial plants, best in the sense that their control procedures, with respect to their effluents, represented the "best practical control technology currently available."

After much review of the available evidence, EPA published tentative regulations and provided an opportunity for both industry and the general public to comment. The process of issuing final regulations soon became an iterative one between the Agency and industry. For example, in the pulp and paper industry, EPA published "preliminary proposed regulations" for five industry subcategories on July 13, 1973, and received much feedback from both industry and the public. On January 15, 1974, they published "proposed regulations," and once again much discussion ensued. On May 29, 1974, they issued effluent guideline "regulations" for each of the five subcategories. These generated still more discussion, mainly over the issue that the five industrial subcategories were insufficient to describe the variety of processes within the pulp and paper industry. As a result, EPA added 15 additional subcategories on September 5, 1975, and invited additional comments. Final regulations are still in the making. Similar histories exist for other industry categories and subcategories.

Many changes in effluent standards are brought on by this iterative process. For example, the BPT standards for BOD_5 for the initial five subcategories of the pulp and paper industry are displayed in Table C.1. New data and arguments supplied by industry persuaded the Agency to raise effluent standards to higher (that is, more relaxed) levels. When the BPT effluent limitations for the additional subcategories of the pulp and

TABLE C.1 BOD_5 Effluent Limitations BPT Pulp and Paper Industry

Industry Subcategories	Maximum for Any One Day				
	A	B	C	D	E
Proposed 15 Jan 74, 39 FR 1908	4.0	4.5	8.75	6.35	2.2
Ordered 29 May 74, 39 FR 18742	5.6	8.7	8.0	8.0	3.0

Industry Subcategories	Maximum Average of Daily Values for Any Thirty Consecutive Days				
	A	B	C	D	E
Proposed 15 Jan 74, 39 FR 1908	2.2	3.25	5.25	3.05	1.25
Ordered 29 May 74, 39 FR 18742	2.8	4.35	4.0	4.0	1.50

paper industry were published, the same pattern of changes occurred, as illustrated in Table C.2. Similar changes in effluent standards can be documented for most industries. The establishment of environmental regulations is clearly an iterative process, heavily dependent on the adequacy of data resources.

SOME USES OF STATISTICS IN ESTABLISHING STANDARDS

The establishment of a water effluent standard for a particular industry subcategory follows a general pattern, although many variations occur. The first task faced by the Agency is to identify those industrial plants whose treatment of their pollution effluents represents the "best practical control technology currently available." Such plants are usually chosen for engineering reasons related to their performance quality. The determination of an effluent guideline next requires the compilation of data histories obtained from these BPT plants. The data on pollution measures, when gathered into a histogram, commonly display two characteristics: (1) a skewed-to-the-right distribution; and (2) occasional "outlier" observations falling far beyond the usual range of the histogram. Ordinarily, these outlying observations are purged and other observations are frequently deleted because of bias in the measuring instruments, or ancillary information indicating that the data are not representative. This laundering of the data bank entails the use of some statistical tools, but in practice, the essential laundering is performed for other reasons, the use of statistical arguments providing only a minor portion of the overall rationale. These data exclusions limit the mathematical modeling and guideline construction to standard steady-state plant operating conditions, and are the source of much discussion between the Agency and industry.

Often, the next step is to transform the observations in such a way that that their histogram becomes symmetric and easily characterized by a Gaussian distribution. The usual transformation chosen is the logarithm of the data, that is, $z = \ln y$, although other transformations have been proposed. The decision to transform the data, and the choice of transformation, is left to the statistical analyst. The resulting distribution is then taken to represent observations from plants employing the "best practicable control technology currently available."

Formal attention is now given to the incorporation of uncertainty into the establishment of an effluent regulation for an industrial plant. As is well known, given observations from a Gaussian distribution with mean η and variance σ^2 both known, the probability of a single observation

TABLE C.2 BOD$_5$ Limitations BPT Pulp and Paper Industry

Maximum for Any One Day

Industry Subcategories

	L	M	N	O	P	F	G	H	I	J	K	Q	R	S	T	U	V
Proposed 5 Sept 75, 40 FR 41300	5.95	4.4	7.1	6.35	9.75	21.95	12.05	10.75	7.9	25.75	38.5	11.9	07.1	07.9	07.9	–	–
Interim 19 Feb 76, 41 FR 7662	13.5	9.6	8.55	7.7	13.5	25.65	15.2	13.35	10.95	37.6	42.9	18.15	8.2	11.4	12.3	52.3	1.1

Maximum Average of Daily Values for Any Thirty Consecutive Days

Industry Subcategories

	L	M	N	O	P	F	G	H	I	J	K	Q	R	S	T	U	V
Proposed 5 Sept 75, 40 FR 41300	3.5	2.6	4.2	3.75	5.75	12.95	12.05	6.35	4.7	15.2	22.7	7.0	4.2	04.7	04.7	–	–
Interim 19 Feb 76, 41 FR 7662	7.05	5.0	4.45	4.0	7.2	13.35	15.2	6.95	5.7	19.6	22.35	9.45	4.25	06.25	06.4	26.3	0.55

falling beyond the boundary $\eta+3\sigma$, the "3 sigma limits" equals 0.00135. Such an event is considered so rare, that should it occur, the decision is made that the plant is not operating properly and is in violation of the effluent regulation.

The mean of the available observations, η, is estimated by computing their average $\bar{z}=\Sigma z/n$, and the variance of the observations σ^2 is estimated by the statistic $s^2=\Sigma(z-\bar{z})^2/(n-1)$, where n is the number of available observations. Given z and s^2, the Agency has often established the upper boundaries for single observations at $\bar{z}+3s$. ("Single" observations frequently represent the average performance over a day's production.)

Of course, if exact knowledge of either the mean η or variance σ^2 is unavailable, an estimate of the boundary beyond which only x percent of the observations will lie, that is, the "tolerance limit," is required. A boundary equal to $\bar{z}+Ks$ can be constructed so that an analyst can say with some confidence that the boundary excludes the upper x percent of the observations. The factor K is tabulated in the statistical literature, but is seldom employed by the Agency.

Another approach used by the Agency is to compute a "variability factor," $v=(z+3s)/z$. This factor is used to convert a plant's average performance over a year's time, y, into a limit for daily observations by computing vy.

Still another approach is to take the observations, place them in order of magnitude, and plot them on probability paper. An estimate of the median and the 99th percentile is then obtained from the plot, and the variability factor V is determined by:

$$V = \frac{\text{99th percentile}}{\text{50th percentile}}$$

and used as an estimate of $(\eta+3\sigma)/\eta$. Given V and the long-term average performance of a plant, y, the upper guideline limit for daily observations is given by Vy.

Effluent limitations are also quoted for 30-day averages. These limits are sometimes constructed from historical collections of 30-day averages (or monthly averages) obtained from the acceptable plants. (Often the monthly "averages" are merely single observations recorded once each month by the plant.) It is common to set the upper bound on the 30-day averages at $\bar{z}+2s$. The variability factor for monthly 30-day averages would then be $v=(z+2s)/\bar{z}$, where both $\bar{z}$ and s^2 are computed from the 30 day data. On other occasions, the Agency has established 30-day upper bounds by using some fraction of the computed daily upper bounds, or vice versa.

It is clear that the Agency uses statistical tools in various ways to determine the BPT bounds for NPDES permits. But our description of how the bounds are determined has been idealized. Often, no data on pollution levels are available for an industrial subcategory. In this circumstance, the Agency has generated data in a very short period of time, and under what were hopefully representative operating conditions. On other occasions, special visits to acceptable plants were made, and operating data secured from which pollution data could be inferred.

In a few situations, long historical records were available, and statistical analysis played a dominant role in determining effluent limitations. Even here, however, there was much discussion over whose data should be used, which observations laundered, what transformation employed, and so on.

Furthermore, there has almost always been a lack of truly acceptable baseline data. The Agency needs long historical records of pollution measurements made by BPT plants under programs of measurement quality assurance. With such records, it is certainly possible to establish daily limits and limits for 30-day averages in keeping with sound statistical practice. Instead, the Agency is usually faced with a dearth of data, or with accumulations of data of poor quality. Without good baseline data, considerations of uncertainty and discussions of the statistical aspects of many BPT limits become academic. Hopefully, much better data will be available for analysis when the time arrives to review current regulations.

STATISTICAL PROBLEMS IN ESTABLISHING STANDARDS

It will be helpful to identify in greater detail some of the statistical problems associated with the establishment of environmental guidelines and standards, and with the making of decisions under uncertainty. We begin by asking the reader to study Figure C.1, which illustrates the changing level of concentration of a pollutant entering the environment from a single source. The wandering line labeled η is the true pollutant response level plotted against time. Of course, at any point in time, t, an actual recorded observation will not equal η but differ from η by a random "error" or "disturbance." The recorded observation at time t is illustrated by the point y on the figure. The curve that represents the distribution of possible observations at a specific time t is chosen to be Gaussian (normal) and should be viewed as vertical to the page. Also plotted on the figure is a "critical boundary," an environmental regulation or limit. Any observation falling above this critical boundary is taken as prima-facie evidence of noncompliance and carries with it reprimands and possible fines.

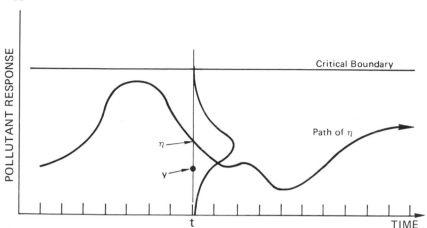

FIGURE C.1   The time plot of the true level of the pollutant and associated upper critical boundary.

There are three models evident in Figure C.1. The first concerns the level of pollution response η; the second the distribution of the disturbances that give rise to the observations y; and the third concerns the effects of η upon some health or environmental response leading to the establishment of the critical boundary.

The practical problem is complicated by the fact that none of these three models is known by the analyst, and each model must be inferred from an observed data trace, as illustrated in Figure C.2. Our analysis begins with the data in Figure C.2 and the concepts of the problem given in Figure C.1.

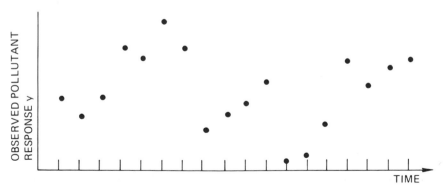

FIGURE C.2   The time plot of observed values of the pollutant.

When such data have been analyzed in the past, the level of the response η is usually considered to be a constant, and the entire collection of observations to be represented by a marginal histogram, as illustrated in Figure C.3. These data are then used to identify and characterize the distribution of the disturbances. In this simple example, the Gaussian distribution seems to be a good candidate, and it would thus be possible to determine the average, y, and estimate of variance, s^2, and to use these two statistics to identify a boundary beyond which only a very small percentage of future observations would be expected to occur. In keeping with EPA practice, this boundary has been set at $y + 3s$ in the figure. We note that in this analysis little has been assumed about the effect of the pollutant on any environmental or health response, except that high values are bad. The boundary has been set using statistical arguments coupled with a simplistic model, and based on data chosen for engineering reasons. Given data such as that illustrated in Figure C.2, there is little more that can be done.

ASSUMPTIONS CONCERNING η

In the analyses used to establish BPT limits, the response η is commonly assumed to be constant and all observed variation in the observations, y, assigned to random disturbances. Daily and seasonal variations in η are always possible, however, and the manufacturing process may produce gradual changes. One consequence, when η varies, is that the shape of the distribution of observations is determined not only by the measurement variability, but also by the length of time η remains at any one level. The distortion of the shape of the distribution of observations caused by changes in the level of η can be serious, and can easily lead to the establishment of BPT limits that are unnecessarily high and are not a function of manufacturing control technology. In the future, in establishing regulations, greater efforts should be made to take into account the possibility that η varies over time. Furthermore, the Agency should adjust effluent limitations to reflect the manufacturer's ability to control the process at any given point in time.

The ability to determine the varying path of η depends on how often its time trace is sampled. Manufacturing requirements now largely determine this sampling frequency. If the effects of η on some environmental response could be quantified, or the cost that attends departures from control estimated, then alternative sampling frequencies might be called for. If good data on effects and cost existed, the Agency would be able to adapt the frequency of sampling to match requirements of environmental management.

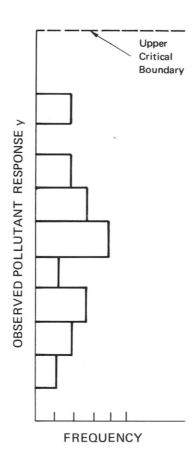

FIGURE C.3   Histogram of observations.

Of course, η is not always a constant or even a smoothly varying function: production upsets, spills, shutdowns, and other events, provide discontinuities. Many "outlier" observations are undoubtedly due to process discontinuities, and their number, magnitude, and location in time provide important information on the quality of pollution control. Outlier observations should therefore not be mechanically purged from a data record, but set aside and carefully studied.

ASSUMPTIONS CONCERNING THE DISTURBANCES

When the response η is observed, the act of taking an observation always entrains a disturbance, that is, any recorded observation y is assumed to be of the form $y = \eta + \epsilon$, where η is the actual value of the respose and ϵ is a disturbance brought about by the measurement process. Given that η is a constant, it is usually assumed that the variability due to the disturbances is such that the magnitude and sign of each disturbance is not dependent on the magnitude and sign of any other. Further, it is commonly assumed that the distribution of these disturbances is well characterized by a Gaussian distribution located at η, is stable, and has a constant variance σ^2.

Adequate control of the variance of the measurement process is essential. The usual assumption is that σ^2 is a constant, but it may be constant and so large that it permits nothing but the broadest limits on the observed pollutants. When the variance is large, special studies aimed at identifying the components of the variance are necessary, and programs of quality assurance are required to guarantee control over the variance. If the variance σ^2 is not constant only careful studies are likely to reveal the facts. EPA has conducted components of variance studies and quality assurance programs Agency in the past, some programs demonstrating much sophistication. As the need to standardize the measurement process across the nation increases, many more such programs will be required. It will be important for the Agency to expand in-house capacity both to design and analyze these efforts.

The measurement process must also be stable, that is, the basic characteristics of the distribution must be invariant over time, and the number and nature of maverick observations must not be so large or so unusual as to force the data analyst to lose confidence in the measurement method itself. The absence of stability or the lack of measures of precision and interlaboratory bias makes it almost impossible to write statistically valid effluent limitations.

THE INCORPORATION OF UNCERTAINTY

When the measurement process is stable, Gaussian, with both η and σ^2 constant and known, it is easy to determine the proportion of observations that will exceed any fixed boundary. As indicated earlier, the Agency often establishes this boundary at the "3 sigma limits" so that, given the validity of the assumptions, it will be exceeded by a single observation with a probability of only 0.00135. Regulations usually state, however, that the polluter will "never" exceed such boundaries; if he does, he will be in violation of regulations and subject to penalty. But obviously, there is a probability of 0.00135 that he will violate the regulation's upper boundary. Nevertheless, even though we cannot be certain of the true level of the pollution response (because of the errors of measurement), we take the decision, under uncertainty, that a violation has occurred whenever an observation exceeds the boundary. On those rare occasions when an acceptable process is declared to be in violation, a Type I Error is declared. The Agency attempts to keep the probability of a Type I error low, with the smallest value equal to 0.00135 and the largest value approximately 0.05.

In establishing effluent guidelines, the Agency has said little about the "Type II Error," that is, the decision to declare the process acceptable when it is not. In explanation, suppose that η is located on the critical boundary. Acceptance of the process with η at such a high a level would be most unwelcome in many circles. However, given that the disturbances were symmetrically distributed, half the observations would lead the decision maker to declare the process acceptable; the Type II error would occur with a probability of 0.5. Effluent limits and sampling requirements established by the Agency usually do not consider the Type II Error. Well known methods are available for insuring that both types of errors of decision making under uncertainty are small. The cost of programs designed to keep the Type I and Type II errors small is almost always an increase in the number of samples.

In the real world of determining BPT limitations, and long before formal consideration of Type I and Type II errors is possible, the major practical difficulty is getting parties to agree on a single acceptable data set. This problem should gradually diminish in importance as the measurement processes for pollutants come under control. We look forward to the day when environmental sampling plans can be established with recognition of the problems of making decisions under uncertainty.

In the work of the Agency, even when good data are available, careful documentation of the assumptions and calculations is often lacking. It should always be possible, given the identical data set and confidence level, for statisticians outside the Agency to repeat the computations and obtain the boundaries reported, as supported by the data. When nonstatistical arguments are brought to bear on the establishment of pollution limitations, these factors should be explicitly stated.

DEPARTURES FROM DISTRIBUTION ASSUMPTIONS

The establishment of an effluent guideline, and the resulting decision procedures, depend heavily upon the assumptions underlying the measurement process. When the process can be assumed to be Gaussian with both η and σ^2 constant, it is easy to determine the probability that an observation will exceed a given boundary.

But when an observed histogram of observations characterizing the measurement process is not Gaussian-like, or more importantly not symmetric, difficulties ensue, and data transformations may have to be employed to obtain a more symmetric distribution. If we grant that η is a constant, the essential contribution to non-Gaussian appearing histograms lies with the choice of the measurement metric. Such metrics should be transformed, and one chosen which gives a Gaussian-like distribution. Computations and estimates should be performed in this new metric, and only at the end should results be transformed back to the naive or arbitrary metric of the data taker. The use of non-symmetrical distributional forms, accompanied by long discussions on how to estimate essential parameters and to determine probability statements, cloud the essential issue that simplicity works. If by a simple transformation, the data can be made to appear symmetric (and, it is hoped, nearly Gaussian), the transformation should be employed without undue apologies.

There are cases in which other distributional forms are required. Upsets in process performance may be characterized by the Poisson distribution, some error regimes are naturally double exponential, and some result from the use of special statistics posing as single observations. The use of distributional forms other than the Gaussian should be supported by information beyond that contributed by the immediate histogram under study. The Agency is urged not to proliferate the types of distributions it employs in establishing effluent limits.

ASSUMPTIONS CONCERNING EFFECTS DUE TO η

The establishment of upper bounds for pollutant levels requires a model associating the pollutant, as a cause, to some effect in the environment. The simplest model is to declare that more of anything called a pollutant is bad, and less is better. This model is certainly humble, and avoids the need to quantify a cause-and-effect relation. It has provided a basis for the establishment of a pollution control policy as evidenced by the BPT and BAT limitations, and the associated NPDES permit program. A current question is how to improve the future performance of the Agency under this model.

The answer lies in establishing a data base which describes the extent of pollution control that well run industries can really achieve, and in employing appropriate statistical methods to extract the information in these data. The NPDES data on effluents are inadequate for this purpose.

The data are taken by industry under measurement method quality assurance programs of uncertain character. The frequency of sampling is often minimal, and data reporting is not timely. Further, the data are taken to meet the objectives of regulation enforcement. This objective is necessary, but it produces information of little value in learning how processes actually work. The accumulation of data bases descriptive of excellent performance will require an active program on the part of the Agency.

The construction of models that relate the pollution level of η to environmental responses is just beginning. A grave danger here is that it is easy to construct empirical models relating supposed causes and effects when large data banks of data are available. The inference of causation and the construction of models should not be based solely on post hoc studies, but rather should be the result of carefully stated hypotheses and well planned programs of data collection and experimentation. The Agency has encouraged such studies and should do more of them.

INDEPENDENCE

In all of the discussions concerning the establishment of environmental guidelines and standards given above, the individual observations have been assumed to be independent. This means that each disturbance has certain essential probabilistic characteristics. In lay terms, the magnitude and sign of any disturbance is not predictable in any way from the magnitude and sign of any other disturbance. More formally, the probability associated with disturbance A when multiplied by the probability of disturbance B equals the probability that both disturbances A and B occur. The analyst's assumptions about independence are most important to the analysis of environmental data. For example, if sequential data collected on pollutants were independent, it would be quite unnecessary to institute separate studies to establish both one-day and 30-day limitations.

In almost all the analyses used by the Agency for setting guidelines, the model assumed for the response η is that it is a constant, and the model assumed for the disturbances, whatever distributional form is chosen, is that they are independent. Usually, neither model is valid. In fairness to the Agency, given the poor quality of the data bases available, these assumed models are at least a place to begin. But with the advent of better data, assumptions concerning the time path of η and the independence of the observations will have to be stated and checked.

MODELS AND DATA

We note that it is impossible to separate modeling from data gathering. They share mutually iterative roles, changes in proposed models generating new data requirements, and new data producing information which leads to modification of previously held models. Further, there is no single prescription for postulating models or their associated data requirements. What models and data are appropriate to the Agency in meeting its responsibilities to understand and manage the environment will depend on the Agency's priorities. If the effluent at an industrial plant is only of slight economic or social importance, all that is needed is a simple statement of the effluent limitation, modest surveillance, and an occasional check to determine whether the instrumentation and record keeping are in good order. In this circumstance, the data needs are slight, and the simple models of constant response and independent observations are adequate. But if the response is significant, or the industry is a major polluter, then much more sophisticated data requirements, models, and effluent limitations are likely to be called for. Both the varying character of the response η and the stochastic structure of the disturbances may need to be considered. Further, the effect of η upon the environment should be stated clearly. The costs for surveillance and for additional information and analyses must, in any case, be weighed against the benefits.

CONCLUSION

The establishment of environmental guidelines and standards has proved to be an iterative process. Historically, the Agency has proposed regulations and standards, and both industry and the public have subsequently brought new data and arguments to light, which led to the modification of these regulations. We found the use of statistical procedures in the establishment of these regulations and standards to be largely ad hoc. Where appropriate data were available, the Agency established regulations using statistical principles that control the Type I Error, that is, the error of declaring an acceptable process to be in violation. Control of the Type II Error, the probability of declaring a bad process to be acceptable, has been largely neglected. Serious consideration of the cost of taking decisions under uncertainty, particularly the wrong decisions, is destined to have a dramatic effect upon the size and nature of sampling requirements necessary to meet regulations.

In many cases, the Agency lacks data of adequate quality and quantity to be useful for establishing regulations. With such poor raw material, the ability of the Agency to progress much beyond the simplest applications of statistical methods is limited. However, as new and better data resources become available, as a consequence of the Agency's quality assurance programs, the Agency will wish to apply better modes of statistical analysis. The Agency should prepare for these future events by establishing centers of excellence in both the practice and theory of statistics. Simultaneously, the Agency should use its current scant statistical resources only to solve those problems identified as most important to the Agency. This may require separating statistical needs into activities to be performed in-house, and those to be handled by outside statisticians. For example, we can imagine special in-house efforts in the establishment of regulations and environmental modeling, in forensic statistics, and in quality assurance, while the technical considerations of establishing sampling networks and protocols, the study of the influence of departures from statistical assumptions, and the adaptation of multivariate and time series methodologies to environmental problems might be contracted out to various universities or groups with special statistical expertise.

The Agency should take a more global view of its statistical needs and responsibilities and prepare for vigorous, organized growth.

D Directories of Monitoring Programs and Monitoring Information Centers

GENERAL

GLOBAL

Strategic Environmental Planning (1974) Directory of National and International Pollution Monitoring Programs. P.O. Box 162, Concord, Mass. 01742.

> Directory in the form of a computer printout which lists 700 long-term programs including 141 in the United States. Gives name, address, access to data, pollutant monitored, physical medium, geographical area, measurement techniques, and sampling frequency. May be updated every three years. Includes indexes for pollutant and medium. About $100. 1859 pp. Contact: John Whitman. (617) 369-8480.

United Nations Environment Program (1974) Directory of National and International Pollution Monitoring Programs. Three Vols. Cambridge, Mass.: Smithsonian Institution, Center for Short-Lived Phenomena. 1272 pp.

Wilson, W.K., M.D. Dowd, and P. Sholtys, eds. (1974) World Directory of Environmental Research Centers. 2nd Ed. sponsored by the Lake Erie Environmental Studies (LEES) Program. Scottsdale, Ariz.: Oryx Press (Distributed by R.R. Bowker). 330 pp.

154

Brief listings include address, director's name, and special interests of the center (forest, aquatic, etc.). Organized by subject (biology, chemistry, engineering, etc.) and by country.

NATIONAL (U.S.)

Council on Environmental Quality (1973) The Federal Environmental Monitoring Directory. Washington, D.C.: Council on Environmental Quality. 105 pp.
Limited to programs operated by federal agencies. Divided into sections on population, food, pollution, ecological factors, and land use.

Paulson, G.L., J.Y. Willen, R.S. Anderson, K.R. Greenhall, L. Paulson, and L. Slesin, eds. (1974) Environment U.S.A.: A Guide to Agencies, People, and Resources. New York: R.R. Bowker. 432 pp.
General handbook of names, addresses, and programs of agencies, environmental groups, industries, and professional organizations.

Strategic Environmental Planning (1974) Directory of U.S. Pollution Monitoring Programs. P.O. Box 162, Concord, Mass. 01742.
Directory in the form of a computer printout which lists 141 U.S. programs, also contained in the Directory of National and International Pollution Monitoring Programs described above. About $40. 356 pp. Contact: John Whitman. (617) 369-8480.

Thibeau, C.F. and P.W. Taliaferro, eds. (1972) NFEC Directory of Environmental Information Sources. 2nd ed. Boston, Mass.: The National Foundation for Environmental Control, Inc. (Distributed by Cahners Books). 457 pp.
Sections entitled: U.S. Government (Executive Agencies, Legislative Committees, Independent Agencies); Citizens Organizations; Published Bibliographies; Conferences and Proceedings; Books; Film Strips; etc. Topical index. Addresses, directors, public information contacts; little technical detail.

U.S. Energy Research and Development Administration (1976) Environmental Monitoring at Major U.S. Energy Research and Development Administration Contractor Sites, 1975. Two Vols. Washington, D.C. 1501 pp.
Includes monitoring results for air, surface and ground water, drinking water, food, wildlife, soil, and vegetation: radioactivity, radionuclide concentrations, and nonradiological pollutants. Also human radiation exposure rates, including whole body dose to entire population within 50 mile radius of site.

U.S. Environmental Protection Agency, Libster, L., comp. (1976) Environmental Information Systems Directory. Management Information and Data Systems Division. Washington, D.C.: U.S. Environmental Protection Agency. 105 pp.

Describes 45 of EPA's larger (over $20,000 computer costs) monitoring data banks and information systems. The purpose, annual cost, primary users, responsible persons, and mode of operation are described. Information on parameters measured, techniques, frequency, etc. is not included. For management purposes.

U.S. Environmental Protection Agency (1973) Environmental Information Systems Directory. Management Information and Data Systems Division. Washington, D.C.: U.S. Environmental Protection Agency. 111 pp.

A comprehensive listing of about 280 of EPA's manual and automated information systems. Some overlap with 1976 version. Air, water, pesticides, noise, solid waste, and miscellaneous categories. Indices of administrative and environmental mission support systems.

U.S. Environmental Protection Agency (1976) National Directory of Sources of Environmental Information in the United States Registered with the United Nations Environment Program International Referral System. UNEP/IRS. U.S. International Environmental Referral Center. Washington, D.C.: U.S. Environmental Protection Agency.

Descriptions of information centers and monitoring programs of over 600 sources in the United States. Source information includes address of responsible office, sponsoring organization, community of responsibility, activities, subjects covered, geographical area, language, format, and conditions under which information will be made available. Sources include 30 percent federal agencies, 18 percent universities, 15 percent industry, 8 percent local and state governments, 29 percent professional organizations, societies, consultants. Subject, source, title, and geographical indices.

Wolff, G.R., ed. (1974) Environmental Information Sources Handbook. New York: Simon and Schuster. 568 pp.

Five sections entitled National Civic and Conservation Groups, Engineering and Professional Societies, Industry Associations, Commercial Newsletters and Information Sources, and Offices and Agencies of the Federal Government. Short descriptions of each organization are given, but no detailed information on individual monitoring programs.

STATE AND LOCAL

Smithsonian Institution (1974) State Environmental Inventory Activities: A Guide to Individuals, Information Sources, and Selected Literature in Forty-four States. Prepared by the Office of International and Environmental Programs, Center for Natural Areas, for the Office of Chief of Engineers, Department of the Army. Washington, D.C.: U.S. Corps of Engineers. 1028 pp.

> State-by-state descriptions of environmental departments and divisions. Descriptions of individual programs; print-outs of personnel. Divided into such categories as Ecological Systems, Conservation and Natural Resources, Coastal Zone, Soils, etc. Includes 43-page master list of literature (largely state agency planning and management studies) by lead author.

U.S. Environmental Protection Agency (1973) Directory of State Agencies Engaged in Environmental Monitoring. Office of Research and Development. Washington, D.C.: U.S. Environmental Protection Agency. 82 pp.

U.S. Environmental Protection Agency (1975) Directory of EPA, State and Local Environmental Quality Monitoring and Assessment Activities. Office of Research and Development. EPA 600/4-75-001. Washington, D.C.: U.S. Environmental Protection Agency; PB-241 757. Springfield, Va.: National Technical Information Service.

> Summaries of EPA, state, and local monitoring activities by state for air quality (six pollutants, frequency of sampling, and number of samples); water programs (about 43 pollutants, number of stations observing over five years); interstate water carrier supplies; pesticides; radiation; noise; and solid waste. May be updated in 1977. Contact: Technical Information Division, EPA. Attn. Ms. Smith.

TOPICAL

AIR

U.S. Environmental Protection Agency (1972) Air Quality Data: Directory of Air Quality Monitoring Sites, 1971. Office of Air Programs, APTD-0979. Research Triangle, N.C.: U.S. Environmental Protection Agency; PB-223 600/8GA. Springfield, Va.: National Technical Information Service. 153 pp.

U.S. Environmental Protection Agency (1975) Directory of Air Quality Monitoring Sites Active in 1973. Monitoring and Data Analysis Division.

EPA-450/2-75/006. Research Triangle Park, N.C.: U.S. Environmental Protection Agency; PB 246 659. Springfield, Va.: National Technical Information Service.

HEALTH

U.S. Department of Health, Education, and Welfare (1975) Health Statistics Plan: Fiscal Years 1976-77. Health Data Policy Committee. Washington, D.C.: U.S. Public Health Service. 125 pp.
  Descriptions of approximately 300 data gathering programs sponsored by HEW; includes information about the design, size, and principal investigator.

PESTICIDES

Federal Working Group on Pest Management (1975) Catalog of Federal Pesticide Monitoring Activities in Effect July 1973. Washington, D.C.: Federal Working Group on Pest Management. 450 pp.
  Describes nine federal pesticide monitoring programs. Lists 16,000 sites, pesticides tested, and frequency of testing at each site.

WATER

Canada Department of the Environment (1973) Index of Water Quality Stations. Inland Waters Directorate, Water Quality Branch. Ottawa, Canada: Department of the Environment. 87 pp.

U.S. Geological Survey (1975) Catalog of Information on Water Data, Edition 1974. Office of Water Data Coordination. Reston, Va. 22092. 21 vols.
  Lists station locations, types of field measurement and types of data collected for streamflow and stage (25,000 stations); quality of surface water (16,300); and quality of groundwater (5700).

U.S. Geological Survey (1975) Digest of the 1974 Catalog of Information on Water Data. Office of Water Data Coordination. Reston, Va. 22092.

MONITORING INFORMATION AND REFERRAL CENTERS

Aerometric and Emissions Reporting System (AEROS) (current) U.S. Environmental Protection Agency, Air Pollution Technical Information Center, Research Triangle Park, N.C. 22151.
  Provides monitoring data and reports based on the following EPA data files: SAROAD (aerometric data); NEDS (emissions data); SOTDAT (stack testing

data); HATREMS (hazardous pollutants); SIPs (full texts of state regulations); EDS (energy); FPC-67 (power plants); EHIS (emissions estimates for previous years); and QAMIS (quality assurance data). Contact: AEROS representatives at EPA Regional Offices.

Environmental Data Index (ENDEX) (current) National Oceanographic Data Center, NOAA/EDS, 2001 Wisconsin Avenue, N.W. Washington, D.C. 20235.

Provides descriptions of about 7800 environmental data bases mostly in Great Lakes and coastal areas: institution holding the data, type and amount of data, geographic area, collection methods, etc. Individualized searches performed. Contact: Christopher Noe. (202) 634-7298.

National Inventory of Biological Monitoring Programs (current) Biological Monitoring Inventory, Environmental Sciences Division, Oak Ridge National Laboratory, Oak Ridge, Tenn. 37830.

This computerized inventory provides descriptions of more than 1000 biological monitoring programs and over 2000 baseline studies. Each program and study is described in detail and includes funding level, ecosystem or biome type, major type of organism studied, and statistical information. Key word searches performed and print-outs available. Contact: Jack Kemp.

National Water Data Exchange (NAWDEX) (current) NAWDEX Program Office, U.S. Geological Survey. Reston, Va. 22091.

Referral center for collectors and users of data on both surface and groundwater. Contains information on approximately 320 organizations, and an index of data collected at 65,000 sites. Information on an additional 300,000 sites will be added in FY 1977. Collectors inform NAWDEX of their water data holdings; NAWDEX refers requestors to appropriate contacts. Includes 51 local assistance centers in most states. User charges vary depending on agency. Contact: Melvin D. Edwards. (703) 860-6031.

Information File on National and International Pollution Monitoring Programs (last update, November 1974; next update scheduled for early 1977) Strategic Environmental Planning. P.O. Box 162, Concord, Mass. 01742.

Computerized information file on 700 long-term pollution monitoring programs in 78 countries (including 141 U.S. programs). Includes name, address, access to data, pollutant monitored, physical medium, geographical area covered, number of sites, sampling frequency, measurement techniques. Individualized searches made for a fee. No information on calibration in current edition. The information file was to be updated in 1977 and will include calibration information. Contact: John Whitman. (617) 359-8480.

Abstracts of
E Papers in a Supplement
to This Report

The following are abstracts of three papers in a supplement to this report. These papers do not necessarily reflect the views of the Committee. See the notes to Appendix F on the availability of this supplement and other papers of the Study Group on Environmental Monitoring.

ABSTRACT OF QUALITY ASSESSMENT OF MEASUREMENT METHODS
J. Stuart Hunter

Quality Assessment of Measurement Methods (Part 4 of *The Measurement Process*)[1] defines quality assessment for the measurement process as the identification of sources of variability that attend the measurement method, as well as the experimental and statistical evaluation of this variability. There are five essential components of quality assessment.

(1) "RUGGEDNESS TESTS"

A "ruggedness test" of a measurement method is performed by making small changes in several selected factors comprising the analysis protocol. Given an estimate of the variance of the measurement method, those protocol factors that

---

[1] *The Measurement Process* was prepared by J. Stuart Hunter (1977) for the Study Group on Environmental Monitoring. See Appendix F for information about where and how this manuscript can be consulted.

have statistically significant effects can be identified, and the control requirements can be adjusted accordingly.

(2) WORKING STANDARDS FOR THE SELECTION OF A METHOD

Working standards are materials with a known level and precision of response. They provide the benchmarks for comparing different methods and, eventually, for maintaining the calibration of instruments once a method has been chosen.

(3) WORKING STANDARDS TO CHECK ADEQUACY OF METHODS IN
ROUTINE PRACTICE

A test program on actual laboratory performance while following a given protocol usually involves analyses of a standard at 3 to 5 concentration levels, by some 8 to 12 laboratories (industrial, academic, and government) making repeated trial runs on each of several days. The most desirable method is then chosen on the basis of a statistical analysis of the results.

(4) COMPARISONS AMONG LABORATORIES TO CHECK FIELD
PERFORMANCE USING A REAL SAMPLE

Once a method has been chosen, the field performance must be checked by obtaining information concerning the reproducibility of the method and the consistency and bias of the working laboratories. To this end, representative real samples are distributed to the participating laboratories. Biased results are easily identified (for example, by using Youden plots), and steps can then be taken to eliminate the bias in practice.

(5) CONTROL OF THE QUALITY OF DATA WITHIN LABORATORIES

Ongoing surveillance and audit of the processes within a laboratory are required to ascertain whether performance continues to meet specifications. Several different procedures are followed: working samples; routine duplicate experiments; and checks on the statistical stability of the processes.

In addition to the above procedures, quality assurance involves such matters as control of the formation, handling, and protection of documents surrounding the data; management to insure independent judgment on the data; computer handling of the data; and training of personnel.

ABSTRACT OF AMBIENT AIR MONITORING METHODS
John Kinosian

The supplement on ambient air monitoring methods briefly reviews the Clean Air Act and assesses the validity and relevance of each of the Federal Reference Methods (FRM) for measuring concentrations of the six criteria air pollutants, those for which National Ambient Air Quality Standards (NAAQS) exist. The six pollutants are total suspended particulates (TSP), sulfur dioxide (SO_2), nitrogen dioxide (NO_2), carbon monoxide (CO), oxidants, and hydrocarbons. It is concluded that the Federal Reference Methods for sulfur dioxide, nitrogen dioxide, oxidants, and hydrocarbons are faulty and that the one for total suspended particulates is useful only as a surrogate.

The high-vol method for total suspended particulates does not provide any measure of the chemical nature and size distribution of the suspended particles, which are the essential factors in determining visibility and health effects. The reagent specified for sulfur dioxide is unstable at warm temperatures, and the collection efficiency of samplers specified in the nitrogen dioxide method (now revoked) is highly variable. Measurements of sulfur dioxide and nitrogen dioxide may be in error by a factor of three or more. Although the Federal Reference Methods for oxidants may be reliable, the calibration method is inaccurate and reproducibility is poor. In the hands of some users, the GC-flame ionization hydrocarbon analyzers produced data in error of over 100 percent. Furthermore, oxidant and hydrocarbon data used to establish the National Ambient Air Quality Standards were obtained by methods different from the Federal Reference Methods, hence the application of the Federal Reference Methods data for assessing compliance with the National Ambient Air Quality Standards for these pollutants is questionable.

A number of noncriteria pollutants—nitrates, sulfates, and metals in particular—contribute to communitywide pollution problems. Methods for these pollutants need development and standardization on a nationwide basis. The same is true for suspended particulate matter, where methods are needed to measure both particle size distribution and the chemical nature of the particles.

Methods are either lacking or unsatisfactory for monitoring the thousands of chemicals that potentially affect man and his environment. It is not clear whether these potential pollutants can or should be extensively monitored. Special studies conducted near sources of these pollutants may be called for.

Thus, there is a great need for better methods for measuring the criteria pollutants, and for new methods to measure other important and potential pollutants. Quality assurance programs are needed to quantify the limits of error for all data accepted and published by the Environmental Protection Agency. Caution should be exercised in revising or replacing National Ambient Air Quality Standards or measurement methods.

ABSTRACT OF PERSONAL AIR QUALITY MONITORS
Lance Wallace

Data on individual exposure to air pollutants are required, not only to determine high-risk subgroups of the population, but also (in conjunction with studies of health effects) to produce dose-response curves. Although this need has been recognized for about a decade, and development of personal air samplers urged in many major reports on environmental health research needs, EPA is making no effort to develop such devices.

Although it is sometimes argued that measurements at fixed stations coupled with interpolation models can provide adequate estimates of exposure, many studies have revealed great differences between values measured by ambient fixed station monitors and measurements made at breathing zones. Several epidemiological studies used personal monitors; again, important differences were found between personal doses and ambient concentrations.

A survey of some industries that manufacture air pollution measuring equipment found ten that had done research or development work on a variety of personal monitors capable of detecting pollutants at ambient levels. Estimates of the additional investment necessary to produce reasonably priced monitors, in quantity, ranged from $250,000 to $500,00 per device per pollutant. However, no industries were presently planning further research or development, citing the lack of a market as a reason.

An EPA study of the feasibility of personal monitors describes ten different methods. The study selected dual cathode liquid electrolyte amperometry as the preferred method. Moving tape colorimetry was the second choice and chemiluminescence, the third. The study recommended that EPA sponsor forums, inviting university and industry participation, to encourage development of personal monitors.

The Brookhaven Workshop of July 1975 considered a range of promising instrumentation techniques. The Workshop recommended a national investment of $7.5 to $8 million in research and development of personal monitors over the next five years, with parallel development of the most promising technologies before a smaller number are selected for most intensive development.

More precise identification of the population at greatest risk could suggest a less costly and more effective air quality control strategy, thus benefiting both industry and the public. Therefore a strong governmental research and development program, with the possible support of an industrial coalition, is urged.

F
List of
Working Papers

PANEL ON AMBIENT MONITORING

Fiering, Myron B. & Shapiro, Michael (June 1976) Maumee River Case Study [abridged version Appendix B],[1] 25 pp.

Fiering, Myron B. & Walker, William (June 1976) A Case Study of Syracuse/Onondaga Lake,[2] 33 pp.

Goldburg, Walter & Wallace, Lance (July 1976) Dissemination, Public Participation, and Peer Review, 15 pp.

Hunter, J. Stuart (August 1976) Incorporation of Uncertainty into Environmental Guidelines [Appendix C],[3] 30 pp.

Hunter, J. Stuart (August 1976) Siting of Monitoring Measurement Stations, 9 pp.

Hunter, J. Stuart, Muller, Mervin E. & Straf, Miron L. (July 1976) Data and Information Handling Systems, 30 pp.

Kinosian, John (July 1976) Ambient Air Monitoring Methods [Supplement],[4] 41 pp.

Langbein, Walter (July 1976) Design of Water Data Systems, 46 pp.

---

[1]See the appendixes to this report.

[2]Supplements are available in limited quantity, in typewritten form, from the Committee on National Statistics, National Academy of Sciences, Washington, D.C.

[3]See note 1 above.

[4]Working papers not designated as either appendixes or supplements may be consulted by arrangement with the archivist of the National Academy of Sciences, Washington, D.C. There is a charge for retrieving and duplicating manuscripts.

PANEL ON SOURCE MONITORING

Anscombe, F.J. & Hunter, J. Stuart (July 1976) The State of Statistics Within EPA, 15 pp.

Berry, R. Stephen (July 1976) System Evaluation, 20 pp.

Berthouex, Paul M. Monitoring Sewage Treatment Plant Performance, 24 pp. (no date)

Berthouex, Paul M. Monitoring as Material Balance Problem, 10 pp. (no date)

Berthouex, Paul M. Statistical Compatibility in Standards, 15 pp. (no date)

Freed, Virgil (June 1976) Inventory Task, 7 pp.

Freed, Virgil (June 1976) Pesticide Monitoring: Inventory Task, 20 pp.

Freed, Virgil (June 1976) Inventories of Agricultural Pollutants, 3 pp.

Gerstle, Richard (July 1976) Atmospheric Emissions Inventory, 7 pp.

Hunter, J. Stuart (July 1976) Certification of Laboratories, 5 pp.

Hunter, J. Stuart (August 1976) The Measurement Process [Part 4 in Supplement],[5] 79 pp.

Straf, Miron L. (July 1976) Some Comments from the Workshop on Monitoring for Components Behavior Management, 7 pp.

PANEL ON EFFECTS MONITORING

Colwell, Rita (July 1976) Aquatic Systems, 6 pp.

Hamilton, Leonard (April 1976) Individual Air Pollution Monitoring, 7 pp.

Jones, Herbert C. (July 1976) Monitoring of Ecological Effects, 7 pp.

Krueger, Dean (June 1976) Statistical Data on Human Health Effects, 10 pp.

Kuschner, Marvin (July 1976) Cancer, 4 pp.

Kuschner, Marvin (August 1976) Body Burdens, 2 pp.

Neel, James (July 1976) Introduction: Genetics [Appendix A],[6] 16 pp. & 4 tables.

Wallace, Lance (June 1976) The CHESS Story: A Summary of Major Reviews, 32 pp.

Wallace, Lance (October 1976) Occupational Health Statistics, 19 pp.

Wallace, Lance (October 1976) Personal Air Quality Monitors [Supplement],[7] 32 pp. & 2 tables.

Wallace, Lance and Kinlen, Leo (October 1976) Record Linkage, 18 pp.

CONSULTANTS

Klashman, Lester (July 1976) The Inventory Task: Water Pollution, 45 pp.

Kinlen, Leo J. (July 1976) A Review of Methods of Monitoring Health Effects Used in Europe, 80 pp.

Rome, David L. and Whitman, Ira L. (May 1976) A Case Study of Environmental Monitoring in Allegheny County, Pennsylvania, 84 pp.

[5]See note 4 above.
[6]See note 1 above.
[7]See note 4 above.

Biographical G Sketches of Members and Staff of the Study Group

JOHN W. PRATT (*Chairman*) is a Professor in the Graduate School of Business Administration, Harvard University. He received his Ph.D. in statistics from Stanford University in 1956. Dr. Pratt was editor of the *Journal of the American Statistical Association* (1965-1969) and *Statistical and Mathematical Aspects of Pollution Problems* (Marcel Dekker, 1974). His interests include Bayesian decision theory, statistical theory and methodology, and statistical aspects of environmental problems.

FRANCIS J. ANSCOMBE is Professor of Statistics, Yale University. He received his M.A. from Cambridge University in 1943. Professor Anscombe served as chairman for an NRC Advisory Panel for the National Bureau of Standard's Applied Mathematics Division. His expertise is in the fields of statistical methodology and statistical computing.

R. STEPHEN BERRY is a Professor in the Department of Chemistry and a member of the Committee on Public Policy Studies at the University of Chicago. He received his Ph.D. in chemistry from Harvard University in 1956. Dr. Berry served on a National Bureau of Standard evaluation panel on measures for air quality from 1970–73. His research interests are atomic and molecular processes, thermodynamics, resource allocation, energy use, and atmospheric chemistry.

PAUL M. BERTHOUEX is a Professor in the Civil and Environmental Engineering Department of the University of Wisconsin. He is currently Team Leader, Asian Development Bank Project for the Institute of Technology in Surabaya, Indonesia. Dr. Berthouex received his Ph.D. in sanitary engineering at the University of Wisconsin in 1969. His areas of interest include water supply and pollution control, process optimization, modeling and statistical analysis.

RITA R. COLWELL is Professor of Microbiology, University of Maryland. She received her Ph.D. in marine microbiology and marine sciences from the University of Washington in 1961. Dr. Colwell has done research in microbial ecology and systematics, and the use of computers for analysis of microbiological data. She is currently interested in the management of natural resources and the marine environment.

RALPH C. d'ARGE is the John S. Bugas Professor of Economics and Director of the Research and Environmental Economics Laboratory, University of Wyoming. He received his Ph.D. in economics from Cornell University in 1969. Dr. d'Arge's expertise is in the field of resource economics and his current interests include bidding games, adjustment costs, natural resources pricing models, and policy evaluation. Currently, he is managing editor of the *Journal of Environmental Economics and Management* and editor of the *Natural Resources Journal.*

MORRIS H. DeGROOT (*Chairman*, Panel on Ambient Monitoring) is Professor of Statistics, Carnegie-Mellon University. He received his Ph.D. in statistics from the University of Chicago in 1958. Dr. DeGroot is editor of the theory and methods section of the *Journal of the American Statistical Association.* In 1974, he served on a committee appointed by the governor of Pennsylvania to study the health effects of low-level radiation from nuclear reactors.

MYRON B. FIERING is the Gordon McKay Professor of Engineering and Applied Mathematics at Harvard University. He received his Ph.D. in sanitary engineering from Harvard in 1960. Dr. Fiering's interests include water resources, systems analysis, and simulation models for water quality.

VIRGIL H. FREED is Head of the Department of Agricultural Chemistry and Director of the Environmental Health Sciences Center at Oregon State University. He received his Ph.D. in biochemistry from the University of Oregon in 1959. Dr. Freed has done research on the behavior of chemicals in the environment and the metabolism of pesticides and their mode of action. He is particularly interested in the chemodynamics of pesticides and other chemicals in relation to environmental health and quality.

RICHARD W. GERSTLE is the Vice-President of PEDCo-ENVIRONMENTAL, Cincinnati, Ohio. He received his M.S. in chemical engineering from the University of Cincinnati in 1966. Mr. Gerstle has been responsible for projects in air and water pollution assessment and control, waste treatment, cost analyses, development of emission factors, control technology, and regional pollution analyses.

WALTER I. GOLDBURG is Professor of Physics, University of Pittsburgh. He received his Ph.D. in physics from Duke University in 1955. Dr. Goldburg's expertise is in solid state physics. He is interested in the health effects of air pollution and has advised local and state environmental groups.

LEONARD D. HAMILTON is Head of the Biomedical and Environmental Assessment Division and the Office of Environmental Policy Analysis, Brookhaven National Laboratory. He qualified in medicine in 1945 and received his D.M. from Oxford University in 1951 and his Ph.D. in experimental biology from Cambridge University in 1952. Dr. Hamilton's expertise is in health and environmental effects of alternative energy systems, molecular structure of nucleic acids, and function of lymphocytes.

GLENN R. HILST is an environmental consultant for The Research Corporation, Wethersfield, Connecticut. He received his Ph.D. in atmospheric sciences from the University of Chicago in 1957. Dr. Hilst has done research on global monitoring of atmospheric pollution. His current interests are atmospheric transport and chemical conversion of reactive pollutants on a regional and global scale, and chemical reaction rates in turbulent, inhomogeneously mixed systems.

HERBERT C. JONES, III, is Supervisor, Air Quality Research Section, Air Quality Branch, Tennessee Valley Authority. He received his Ph.D. in plant physiology and biochemistry from the University of Florida in 1965. Dr. Jones has had ten years of experience in monitoring and research on the effects of atmospheric emissions from coal-fired power plants, heat dissipation systems, and fertilizer plants on crops and forests. His current interests include the effects of SO_2, mixtures of SO_2 and other air pollutants, and acidic precipitation on crops and forests.

JOHN R. KINOSIAN is Chief, Technical Services Division, California Air Resources Board. He received his B.S. in chemical engineering from the University of California in 1949. Mr. Kinosian's areas of expertise are industrial hygiene and air pollution. He has worked on state air pollution monitoring systems for fifteen years.

DEAN E. KRUEGER is Research Professor, Department of Statistics, George Washington University. He received his M.A. in biostatistics from Columbia University School of Public Health in 1959. Mr. Krueger's interests are in epidemiological methods in the study of chronic diseases, statistical analysis of epidemiological data, and health statistics. His research as Deputy Director of the Office of Health Statistics Analysis at the National Center for Health Statistics included the epidemiology of cardiovascular disease.

MARVIN KUSCHNER (*Chairman*, Panel of Effects Monitoring) is Chairman, Department of Pathology, and Dean, School of Medicine, State University of New York at Stony Brook. He received his M.D. from New York University School of Medicine in 1943. Dr. Kuschner's expertise is in pathology, carcinogenesis, and inhalation therapy. He is currently interested in environmental agents as determinants of disease, particularly pulmonary disease.

WALTER B. LANGBEIN is a hydrologist for the U.S. Geological Survey. He received his B.S. in civil engineering from Cooper Union College in 1931. Mr. Langbein's expertise is in water resources management. He has worked for USGS since 1935. Mr. Langbein is a member of the National Academy of Sciences and a recipient of its G. K. Warren prize for significant advancement in the fields of hydrology and fluviatile geology. He has served on the NRC Geophysics Research Board and Study Committee, and the Panel on Post-Decade Procedures of the U.S. National Committee for the International Hydrologic Decade.

WALTER A. LYON (*Chairman*, Panel on Source Monitoring) is Director, Bureau of Water Quality Management, Pennsylvania Department of Environmental Resources. He received his M.S. in sanitary engineering from the Johns Hopkins University in 1948. Mr. Lyon has worked in water quality planning and management at the local, state, federal, and international level for more than twenty-five years.

BRIAN MacMAHON is Chairman, Department of Epidemiology, Harvard University School of Public Health. He received his Ph.D. in social medicine from the University of Birmingham in 1952 and his M.S. in epidemiology and hygiene from the Harvard University School of Public Health in 1953. Dr. MacMahon's research includes Hodgkin's disease, certain congenital defects, breast cancer, and other cancer epidemiology. He is a member of the Institute of Medicine.

MERVIN E. MULLER is Director, Computing Activities Department, The World Bank. He received his Ph.D. in mathematics from the University of California, Los Angeles, in 1954. Dr. Muller has been engaged in consulting, management, research, and teaching in areas related to computing and statistics since 1950. His current interests include design and evaluation of information systems, statistical experimental designs to aid in the use of simulation models, and the international exchange of technical information on statistical computing.

JAMES V. NEEL is Chairman of the Department of Human Genetics and Professor of Internal Medicine, University of Michigan Medical School. He received his Ph.D. in genetics in 1939 and his M.D. in 1944, both from the University of Rochester. His research interests are population genetics and mutagenesis; he has directed genetic follow up studies in Hiroshima and Nagasaki for the past thirty years. He is a member of the National Academy of Sciences and the Institute of Medicine.

DAVID E. REICHLE is Associate Division Director, Environmental Sciences Division, Oak Ridge National Laboratory. He received his Ph.D. in biological sciences from Northwestern University in 1964. His interests include ecosystem analysis, fate and effects of pollutants in the environment, food chain behavior of toxic contaminants, and ecology of decomposer invertebrates. For the past thirteen years, Dr. Reichle has been involved in research and education in ecosystem ecology and in the development of quantitative ecosystem analysis and its application to problems of environmental quality.

PROFESSIONAL STAFF

MIRON L. STRAF (*Director*) is Research Associate, NRC Committee on National Statistics. Formerly, he was Assistant Professor in the Department of Statistics at the University of California, Berkeley. Dr. Straf received his Ph.D. in statistics from the University of Chicago in 1969. His interests include theoretical and applied statistics and probability theory. He is also Staff Officer for the Panel to Review Statistics on Skin Cancer for the Committee on

National Statistics. Dr. Straf is on leave for 1977–78 at the London School of Economics and Political Science, where he will be Lecturer in Statistics.

J. STUART HUNTER is a Professor in the School of Engineering and Applied Science at Princeton University. He was on sabbatical leave with our study. He received his Ph.D. in statistics from North Carolina State University in 1954. Professor Hunter has also done much industrial consulting and was the founding editor of *Technometrics* in 1959. His expertise is in the fields of applications of statistics in the engineering sciences and statistical design of experiments. He is currently interested in statistical aspects of the measurement of environmental characteristics.

HENDRIK VAN OLPHEN was the Executive Secretary for the NRC Numerical Data Advisory Board. He received his Ph.D. in physical chemistry from Delft Technical University (the Netherlands) in 1951. Dr. van Olphen has studied mine drainage pollution abatement and particulate-organic pollutants interactions in water and soils. He retired from the Academy in March 1977 and is now living in the Netherlands.

LANCE A. WALLACE is now Environmental Scientist, Office of Monitoring and Technical Support, U.S. Environmental Protection Agency. Dr. Wallace received his Ph.D. in astrophysics at the City University of New York in 1973 after which he taught at the Rose-Hulman Institute of Technology. He has written and edited articles on science, technology, and history of science for a number of encyclopedias. His current interests include the linkage of data on the environment and health.

Abbreviations
Used in This Report

AEROS: Aerometric and Emissions Reporting System
ASTM: American Society for Testing and Materials
BAT: Best Available Technology Economically Achievable
BLS: U.S. Bureau of Labor Statistics
BOD: biochemical oxygen demand
BPT: Best Practicable Control Technology Currently Available
CEQ: Council on Environmental Quality
cfs: cubic feet per second
CHAMP: Community Health Air Monitoring Program
CHESS: Community Health and Environmental Surveillance System
CO: carbon monoxide
DO: dissolved oxygen
EPA: U.S. Environmental Protection Agency
ERDA: U.S. Energy Research and Development Administration
FPC: U.S. Federal Power Commission
FRM: Federal Reference Method
FWPCA: Federal Water Pollution Control Administration
FY: fiscal year
GAO: General Accounting Office
GPSF: General Point Source File
LEES: Lake Erie Environmental Studies
MA7CD10: minimum average seven consecutive day low flow
mg/l: milligrams per liter
ml: milliliter
NAAQS: National Ambient Air Quality Standards
NADB: National Aerometric Data Bank

171

NAPCA: National Air Pollution Control Administration
NAS: National Academy of Sciences
NASA: National Aeronautics and Space Administration
NASN: National Air Surveillance Network
NASQAN: National Stream Quality Accounting Network
NAWDEX: National Water Data Exchange
NBS: National Bureau of Standards
NCHS: National Center for Health Statistics
NCI: National Cancer Institute
NEDS: National Emissions Data System
NIH: National Institutes of Health
NIOSH: National Institute for Occupational Safety and Health
NO₂: nitrogen dioxide
NOAA: National Oceanic and Atmospheric Administration
NPDES: National Pollutant Discharge Elimination System
NRC: National Research Council
NSF: National Science Foundation
NQAPLC: National Quality Assurance Program for Laboratory Certification
NWQSS: National Water Quality Surveillance System
OEPA: Ohio Environmental Protection Agency
OMB: Office of Management and Budget
ORSANCO: Ohio River Valley Water Sanitation Commission
OSHA: U.S. Occupational Safety and Health Administration
PARCS: Pesticides Analysis Retrieval and Control System
PCB: polychlorinated biphenyls
ppb: parts per billion
ppm: parts per million
RAMS: Regional Air Monitoring System
RAPS: Regional Air Pollution Study
RFP: request for proposal
SAROAD: Storage and Retrieval of Aerometric Data
SCC: source classification code
SEER: Surveillance Epidemiology and End Results
SIC: standard industrial classification
SIP: state implementation plan
SO₂: sulfur dioxide
STORET: Storage and Retrieval for Water Quality Data
TDS: total dissolved solids
TMACOG: Toledo Metropolitan Area Council of Governments
TPCA: Toledo Pollution Control Agency
TSP: total suspended particulates
UPGRADE: User-Prompted Graphic Data Evaluation
USDA: U.S. Department of Agriculture
USGS: U.S. Geological Survey

Glossary

The definitions in this glossary are intended to help the reader understand some of the scientific terms and monitoring activities mentioned in this report.

Aerometric and Emissions Reporting System (AEROS): EPA's air data management information system that collects, maintains, and reports information describing air quality and emission sources. AEROS resulted from the merging of the National Emissions Data System (NEDS) and the Storage and Retrieval of Aerometric Data (SAROAD) system; it now includes other information systems, such as hazardous air pollutant sources and computerized state air pollution laws and regulations.

Air Quality Control Regions: National regions (247), designated by the federal government, where two or more communities, either in the same or different states, share a common air pollution problem.

Air Quality Criteria Documents: Compilations of the latest available scientific information on the sources, prevalence, and manifestations of recognized air pollutants. They describe the effects that have been associated with, or may be expected from, an air pollutant level in excess of a specific concentration for a specific time period. These effects include: (a) visibility reduction; (b) damage to materials; (c) economic cost; (d) vegetation damage; (e) nuisance aspects; and (f) adverse effects on the health and well-being of man and animals. Air Quality Criteria Documents have been written for the six criteria air pollutants. The research information derived from the documents form the basis of National Ambient Air Quality Standards (NAAQS), which the states are to meet.

aldrin/dieldrin: Chlorinated hydrocarbons used as pesticides with a variety of purposes, from controlling the boll weevil to combating the housefly. Concern over widespread aldrin/dieldrin contamination in the United States and the possibility that they may be a human carcinogen, led EPA to ban nearly all uses of the pesticides in September 1974. They are no longer manufactured in the United States.

allele: One of a number of different forms of a gene. The different alleles of a given gene determine the particular phenotype of the organism.

asbestos: Designated by EPA as a hazardous pollutant under the Clean Air Act in 1975, asbestos is known to cause cancer when inhaled; the effects of ingesting it are unknown. EPA is considering regulation of the manufacture, use, and disposal of asbestos (and its wastes).

benefit–cost analysis: An evaluation of the benefits and costs of a proposed action.

Best Available Technology Economically Achievable (BAT): The second level of a two-level program designed to control and eventually eliminate industrial discharges of pollutants into the nation's waters, established by the Federal Water Pollution Control Act Amendments of 1972. "Best available technology" will be based on the very best control and treatment measures that have been or are capable of being economically achieved. All industries are expected to conform to this level of technology by July 1, 1983.

Best Practicable Control Technology Currently Available (BPT): The first level of a two-level program designed to control and eventually eliminate industrial discharges of pollutants into the nation's waters, established by the Federal Water Pollution Control Act Amendments of 1972. "Best practicable technology" will represent the average of the best existing performances by well operated plants within each industrial category or sub-category. This level of technology is expected to be achieved by all plants no later than July 1, 1977.

bias (of the measurement method): The systematic error of a measurement method; the consistent portion of the deviation of the measured value from the correct value.

biochemical oxygen demand (BOD): A measure of the amount of oxygen consumed in biological processes that break down organic matter in water; a measure of the organic pollutant load. A common measurement, BOD_5, is the amount of dissolved oxygen consumed in five days in oxidation of a residual by bacteria under certain conditions (see dissolved oxygen).

carbon monoxide (CO): An odorless, colorless, toxic gas that acts on blood hemoglobin to reduce the oxygen absorption capacity. It is released by the incomplete combustion of fuels and other carbon-containing substances, such as occurs in motor vehicles. Carbon monoxide is one of the six criteria air pollutants.

carcinogen: A substance that causes cancer in animals or humans.

Chemical Transportation Emergency Center (CHEMTREC): An organization run by the Manufacturing Chemists Association on a 24-hour basis to provide information over the telephone on how to treat chemical spills that result from transportation accidents.

Clean Air Act: Enacted in 1967, the Act embraced the concept that cleaning up the air required a national effort, but specified that states should retain primary authority and responsibility for doing so. The Act was amended in 1970 to provide for development and enforcement of two kinds of standards for ambient air quality—primary standards necessary to protect human health and secondary standards desirable to protect human welfare, including property and aesthetics. The amendments' stated goal was achievement of primary standards throughout the nation between 1975 and 1977. To reach this goal, the amendments set forth a two-part strategy: establishment of air quality standards (see Air Quality Criteria Documents) and development of State Implementation Plans (see heading).

coliform bacteria: A group of organisms common to the intestinal tracts of man and warm-blooded animals. Coliform bacteria is used as an indicator of sanitary quality of water.

Community Health Air Monitoring Program (CHAMP): An EPA program consisting of 23 large, fixed air monitoring stations and 5 mobile units located across the nation to measure ambient concentrations of nitrogen oxides, sulfur dioxide, ozone, hydrocarbons, carbon monoxide, peroxyacetyl nitrate, and total and respirable particulates. These data are used to estimate levels of short-term human exposure, within selected communities, to various air pollutants.

Community Health and Environmental Surveillance System (CHESS): A series of epidemiological studies conducted by EPA in eight U.S. communities from 1969 to 1975. They were designed to investigate effects of specific air pollutants (for example, sulfur oxides and particulates) on the health of particular groups at risk, such as children, asthmatics, and the elderly. The main publication from this program was "Health Consequences of Sulfur Oxides: A Report from CHESS, 1970-1971."

components of error analysis: Analysis of sources of errors. In laboratory observations, errors may be due to differences in sampling, types of analysis, machine operators, number of days, or other factors. By means of designed experiments, the contribution of each component can be estimated.

cost–effective design: The least-cost design to meet some specified goal of accuracy or the most accurate design at a specified cost.

criteria air pollutants: The six major air pollutants for which national ambient air quality standards have been designated: total suspended particulates, sulfur dioxide, carbon monoxide, photochemical oxidants, nitrogen dioxide, and hydrocarbons.

DDT: A pesticide formerly used widely. Because of its persistence in the environment and its ability to accumulate and magnify in the food chain, EPA suspended virtually all uses of DDT in the United States on December 31, 1972.

dissolved oxygen (DO): The amount of oxygen dissolved in a body of water. It is an important indicator of the life-sustaining capacity of water. High levels of DO, 7 to 8 ppm, are necessary for several species of fish. At low levels, 2-3 ppm, only some species, such as carp, are likely to survive.

effluent/emission: Waste material discharged into the environment. Discharges into water are usually referred to as effluents; discharges into air as emissions.

epidemiology: The study of a disease and its causes, especially in relation to the characteristics of those in whom it does and does not occur.

eutrophication: A biological condition in which the productivity of a lake is changed by the overabundance of various nutrients (phosphorous, nitrogen, organic matter). Eutrophication affects the health of aquatic life.

exponentially weighted moving average (EWMA): A statistic that weights the most recent event in time most heavily, and each observation further back in time proportionally less. Observations in the distant past have very little weight.

Federal Water Pollution Control Act: Originally legislated in 1948, this Act sought to protect ambient water quality by relating allowable discharges to the estimated assimilative capacity of the receiving stream or lake. Subsequent amendments broadened the scope of the Act and the 1972 amendments (PL 92-500, which established the National Pollution Discharge Elimination System) tied pollution control to the "best available technology economically achievable" by 1983. The ultimate goal of this latest amendment is to eliminate the discharge of all pollutants into navigable waters by 1985.

gas chromatography: A method of separating and analyzing mixtures of chemical substances. A flow of gas causes the components of a mixture to migrate differentially from a narrow starting zone in a special porous, insoluble, sorptive medium. The pattern formed by zones of separated pigments and of colorless substance in this process is called a chromatogram.

hazardous substance: A substance that, if present in the environment, can pose a danger to human health or ecological well-being. In 16 CFR 1500, hazardous materials or substances are defined to be "any substance or mixture of substances which is toxic, corrosive, an irritant, a strong sensitizer, flammable or combustible, or generates pressure through decomposition, heat, or other means, if such substance or mixture of substances may cause substantial personal injury or substantial illness during or as a proximate result of any customary or reasonably foreseeable handling or use, including reasonably foreseeable ingestion by children."

heptachlor/chlordane: Pesticides similar to DDT and aldrin/dieldrin. The human cancer hazard posed by these pesticides and the lack of benefits to outweigh this risk formed the basis for EPA suspension of most uses in December 1975.

hydrocarbons: A vast family of compounds containing carbon and hydrogen in various combinations, found especially in fossil fuels. Some contribute to photochemical smog. Hydrocarbons are designated as one of the six criteria air pollutants.

karyotype: The chromosome complement of any organism, analyzed according to size and banding patterns of each chromosome.

kepone: A chlorinated hydrocarbon used domestically as an ant and roach poison. In July 1975, Virginia state health officials ordered production of kepone to end, after 70 plant employees were discovered with kepone poisoning. Tests at the National Cancer Institute indicated that kepone caused cancer in laboratory animals.

MA7CD10: Minimum average seven consecutive day flow, occurring once in ten years. This is often taken as the critical flow event for water quality planning.

Market Basket Program: A nationwide survey run by the Food and Drug Administration that samples 117 food items in the basic two-week diet of a 16–19 year old male (statistically the nation's largest eater) to determine pesticide residues.

mass balance: A set of equations representing the indestructibility of material as it flows through a system and which is given by the condition that all the mass (fluid, pollutant, etc.) entering a system during a given time period must leave the system, be stored within the system, or be converted into energy.

mass spectrometry: A procedure for identifying the various kinds of particles present in a given substance, by ionizing the particles and subjecting a beam of the ionized particles to an electric or magnetic field such that the field deflects the particles in angles directly proportional to the masses of the particles.

material balance: See mass balance.

measurement process: A complex of activities associated with the generation of data. The environmental measurement process includes sampling the environment, choosing and applying measurement methods to quantify the environmental parameters under study, and assuring that data are of high quality.

mesothelioma: A rare form of cancer that has become much more common in the past decade; cause of the disease in most victims may be associated with asbestos exposure.

microorganisms: Protozoa, algae, fungi, bacteria, and viruses.

mutagen: A substance capable of causing, within an organism, biological changes that affect potential offspring through genetic mutation. For example, if a pollutant damages a cell but leaves its capacity for division unimpaired, the result may be defects among future generations.

National Aerometric Data Bank (NADB): An EPA data repository that compiles and analyzes air quality data collected primarily by state and local agencies at over 4000 nationwide air monitoring stations.

National Air Surveillance Network (NASN): The principal federal air quality monitoring network. Initiated in the mid-1950s, it currently includes more than 200 monitoring sites generally located in urban areas and operated with state and local cooperation. NASN has accumulated a long-term nationwide record for total suspended particulates and sulfur dioxide.

National Ambient Air Quality Standards (NAAQS): Maximum limits on measures of air pollutant concentrations formulated by EPA for the six criteria air pollutants (total suspended particulates, sulfur dioxide, carbon monoxide, nitrogen dioxide, hydrocarbons, photochemical oxidants). The Clean Air Act Amendments of 1970 require the states to meet these standards. The standards are based on information from EPA's Air Quality Criteria Documents.

National Emissions Data System (NEDS): EPA's data system to compile and analyze data on emissions of air pollutants for each Air Quality Control Region and emissions source category. The data are submitted semiannually by the states.

National Eutrophication Survey: An EPA-conducted survey, from 1972–1975, of 800 of the nation's freshwater lakes and reservoirs to investigate the extent and causes of accelerated eutrophication in these bodies of water (see eutrophication).

National Human Monitoring Program: A program established in 1967 to determine the incidence, levels, and other evidence of exposure to pesticides and PCBs in the general population of the United States. Fatty tissue samples are taken from autopsies and surgical specimens for examination in the program.

National Pollutant Discharge Elimination System (NPDES): A permit system for those who discharge waste into U.S. navigable waters established by the Federal Water Pollution Control Act Amendments of 1972 (see heading). The system requires dischargers (either industries or municipal sewage treatment facilities) to monitor their effluent in order to comply with federal schedules for achieving the optimum water treatment control technology possible by 1983.

National Stream Quality Accounting Network (NASQAN): A network of 345 stations that monitor pollutant concentrations and water flow in a number of planning regions for water resources. It was begun in 1970 by the U.S. Geological Survey.

National Water Data Exchange (NAWDEX): A USGS center for access to information about water data. Ultimately, NAWDEX will provide an index of all water data from various federal agencies, such as EPA, Bureau of Reclamation, Army Corps of Engineers, and ERDA. Until then, it serves primarily as a referral center linking users of water data to collectors.

National Water Quality Surveillance System (NWQSS): Begun in 1974 by EPA, the NWQSS monitors water quality in various areas of the country with distinct land use conditions that affect stream quality. The system is comprised of approximately 70 pairs of monitoring stations, located above and below areas of pollution sources.

nitric oxide (NO): A colorless gas produced during combustion, which reacts in the atmosphere to form nitrogen dioxide.

nitrogen dioxide (NO_2): A brownish-red gas with a pungent odor. Primary sources are atmospheric reactions subsequent to combustion by motor vehicle engines or stationary sources. NO_2 causes aggravation of respiratory and cardiovascular illnesses and is one of the six criteria air pollutants.

ozone (O_3): A pungent, colorless, toxic gas, which is one component of photochemical smog. It also decreases the breaking strength of fibers and causes damage to plants (see photochemical oxidants).

peroxyacetyl nitrate (PAN): A pollutant created by the action of sunlight on hydrocarbons and nitrogen oxides in the air; an integral part of photochemical smog.

Pesticides Analysis Retrieval and Control System (PARCS): The centralized computer system for information on pesticides in the United States, PARCS contains data useful for registration analysis, research, and reporting.

pH: A measure of acidity or alkalinity represented on a scale of 0 to 14, with 7 representing a neutral state; 0, a very strong acid; and 14, a very strong alkali.

phenotypes: The observable characteristics of an organism, resulting from the interaction between an individual's genetic makeup and the environment in which development takes place.

phosphorus: A chemical substance that forms the basis of a large number of compounds, the most important class of which are phosphates. It is absorbed by green plants and used for photosynthesis and metabolism. An excess of phosphorus can cause eutrophication.

photochemical oxidants (O_x): Gaseous compounds that cause other substances to be oxidized. They are produced by the action of light on air and substances in the air. The oxidants are important components of photochemical smog, for example, ozone (O_3), peroxyacetyl nitrate (PAN), aldehydes, and other compounds. Their main health effects are aggravation of respiratory and cardiovascular illnesses, and eye irritation. Oxidants constitute a single category containing many substances, and are designated one of the six criteria air pollutants.

polychlorinated biphenyls (PCB): A family of chlorinated hydrocarbons especially useful as heat transfer fluid, hydraulic fluid, insulating material (in transformers and capacitors), and as a "plasticizer" (an additive to increase flexibility in paints and plastics). They have been found to be highly toxic to aquatic life, to persist in the environment for long periods of time, and to be biologically accumulative. In the recently passed Toxic Substances Control Act (PL 94-469), all uses of PCB are banned within one year of January 1, 1977 (except for use in enclosed containers), and a total prohibition on its manufacture goes into effect in two years.

quality assurance: Managerial activities designed to guarantee the quality of a final product. Examples of these activities are periodic checks on equipment maintenance, the use of interlaboratory tests, compilation of data records, and the training of personnel.

Regional Air Monitoring System (RAMS): An EPA network in the area of St. Louis, Missouri, of 25 air monitoring stations, each equipped with analytical equipment to measure pollutants and meteorological conditions, plus a minicomputer to acquire and transmit data. Sources and types of pollutants will be identifed, as well as the way in which pollutants move through the air and the types of chemical changes that take place under varying conditions.

residual: A quantity of material or energy left over from a production activity. Examples range from waste heat from thermal-electric power generation to fruit and vegetable trimmings in canning.

residual loadings: The amounts of pollutants introduced into the environment (air, water, land) after treatment and management has occurred. Even advanced technology leaves a residual level in the effluent stream.

Safe Drinking Water Act: Effective as of December 16, 1974, the Act calls for primary drinking water standards for substances which may have an adverse effect on human health. Final regulations, however, are not scheduled to be promulgated before September 1977.

sensitivity analysis: Systematic examination of the change in output or system response attributed to small changes in the parameters of a decision-oriented problem. For example, if a number of solutions to a given problem are available, do small changes in parameters of the problem result in new decisions or merely in new values of an objective function?

Spill Prevention Countermeasure Control (SPCC) Plan: A contingency plan prepared by an industry which details the actions to be taken in case oil or hazardous substances are accidentally discharged into a body of water. The plan is submitted to the EPA Regional Administrator and to the state water pollution control authority concerned after the spill has occurred. The Regional Administrator studies the specific case and issues a directive for corrective action in the plan in order to diminish the effect of or to avoid future spills.

Standard Industrial Classification (SIC): Classifies establishments by the type of activity in which they are engaged and covers the entire field of economic activities. The classification was developed for use within the federal government for statistical purposes.

state implementation plan (SIP): A plan which indicates how each state will achieve EPA ambient air quality standards. Typically, each plan is a compilation of state air pollution statutes and regulations and of pollution control strategies—including emission limitations, land use controls, and transportation controls. The plan is submitted to EPA for its approval.

Streeter-Phelps model: A formula for relating the biochemical oxygen demand (BOD) discharged at a particular location in a river to downstream concentrations of dissolved oxygen (DO).

sulfur dioxide (SO_2): A colorless gas with a pungent odor released primarily from the burning of fossil fuels, such as coal, that contain sulfur. It aggravates respiratory illnesses and damages vegetation and materials. One of the six criteria air pollutants.

sludge: The leftover solid waste matter from processing sewage and other wastes.

Storage and Retrieval of Aerometric Data (SAROAD): EPA's computer system for ambient air quality data.

Storage and Retrieval of Water Quality Data (STORET): EPA's computer system for ambient water quality data. It is EPA's largest and most expensive data system with over 30 million observations.

Surveillance, Epidemiology, and End Results Reporting (SEER): A nationwide survey of cancer patients by the National Cancer Institute, the program provides information on the incidence of various forms of cancer; variation in the occurrence of cancer among different population groups, especially those in different geographic areas; changes in diagnostic and treatment practices; and the associated end results.

suspended solids (SS): Small particles of solid pollutants in sewage that contribute to turbidity and resist separation by standard wastewater treatment methods. Along with BOD, suspended solids are used as a measurement of water quality and as an indicator of treatment plant efficiency.

total dissolved solids (TDS): A general term describing the concentration of dissolved materials in water. The more conspicuous constituents of TDS in natural surface waters include carbonates, sulfates, chlorides, phosphates, and nitrates.

total suspended particulates (TSP): Any solid or liquid particles dispersed in the atmosphere, such as dust, pollen, ash, soot, metals, and various chemicals, which have a deleterious effect on human health, impair visibility, and cause deterioration of building materials and other surfaces. One of the six criteria air pollutants.

Toxic Substances Control Act: This legislation, enacted in 1976, requires chemical manufacturers to give EPA up to six months notice before beginning commercial production of a new chemical or manufacturing an existing chemical for a significant new use. If environmental or health information is inadequate or shows possible harm from use of the substance, the EPA Administrator can halt or limit manufacture pending adequate testing of the substance by the company that wishes to produce it. The Act also bans the manufacture of polychlorinated biphenyls (PCBs) within two years.

turbidity: A thick, hazy condition of air due to the presence of particulates or other pollutants, or the similar cloudy condition in water due to the suspension of silt or finely divided organic matter.

User-Prompted Graphic Data Evaluation (UPGRADE): A computerized data system, developed by the Council on Environmental Quality, for analyzing information on the environment, natural resources, public health, and related topics. Thus far, most of UPGRADE's data have been selected from data banks maintained by the U.S. Environmental Protection Agency (SAROAD and STORET), the National Institutes of Health, the National Oceanic and Atmospheric Administration, and the U.S. Geological Survey.

vinyl chloride: A gaseous chemical suspected of causing angiosarcoma, a rare form of cancer of the liver. It is used primarily in the manufacture of polyvinyl chloride plastic.